Ancient India

Other titles in the World History series

Ancient India

Don Nardo

LUCENT BOOKS
A part of Gale, Cengage Learning

GALE
CENGAGE Learning

Detroit • New York • San Francisco • New Haven, Conn • Waterville, Maine • London

© 2008 Gale, Cengage Learning

For more information, contact
Lucent Books
27500 Drake Rd.
Farmington Hills, MI 48331-3535
Or you can visit our Internet site at gale.cengage.com

LIBRARY OF CONGRESS CATALOGING-IN-PUBLICATION DATA

Nardo, Don, 1947–
   Ancient India / by Don Nardo.
      p. cm. — (World history)
   Includes bibliographical references and index.
   ISBN 978-1-4205-0061-5 (hardcover)
   1. India--History--To 324 B.C. 2. India--History--324 B.C.-1000 A.D. I. Title.
   DS451.N29 2007
   934—dc22

                                                          2007037821

ISBN-10: 1-4205-0061-9

Printed in the United States of America
 2 3 4 5 6 7 12 11 10 09 08

Contents

Foreword

Each year, on the first day of school, nearly every history teacher faces the task of explaining why his or her students should study history. Many reasons have been given. One is that lessons exist in the past from which contemporary society can benefit and learn. Another is that exploration of the past allows us to see the origins of our customs, ideas, and institutions. Concepts such as democracy, ethnic conflict, or even things as trivial as fashion or mores, have historical roots.

Reasons such as these impress few students, however. If anything, these explanations seem remote and dull to young minds. Yet history is anything but dull. And therein lies what is perhaps the most compelling reason for studying history: History is filled with great stories. The classic themes of literature and drama—love and sacrifice, hatred and revenge, injustice and betrayal, adversity and overcoming adversity—fill the pages of history books, feeding the imagination as well as any of the great works of fiction do.

The story of the Children's Crusade, for example, is one of the most tragic in history. In 1212 Crusader fever hit Europe. A call went out from the pope that all good Christians should journey to Jerusalem to drive out the hated Muslims and return the city to Christian control. Heeding the call, thousands of children made the journey. Parents bravely allowed many children to go, and entire communities were inspired by the faith of these small Crusaders. Unfortunately, many boarded ships captained by slave traders, who enthusiastically sold the children into slavery as soon as they arrived at their destination. Thousands died from disease, exposure, and starvation on the long march across Europe to the Mediterranean Sea. Others perished at sea.

Another story, from a modern and more familiar place, offers a soul-wrenching view of personal humiliation but also the ability to rise above it. Hatsuye Egami was one of 110,000 Japanese Americans sent to internment camps during World War II. "Since yesterday we Japanese have ceased to be human beings," he wrote in his diary. "We are numbers. We are no longer Egamis, but the number 23324. A tag with that number is on every trunk, suitcase and bag. Tags, also, on our breasts." Despite such dehumanizing treatment, most internees worked hard to control their bitterness. They created workable communities inside the camps and demonstrated again and again their loyalty as Americans.

These are but two of the many stories from history that can be found in the pages of the Lucent Books World History series. All World History titles rely on sound research and verifiable evidence, and all give students a clear sense of time, place, and chronology through maps and timelines as well as text.

All titles include a wide range of authoritative perspectives that demonstrate the complexity of historical interpretation and sharpen the reader's critical thinking skills. Formally documented quotations and annotated bibliographies enable students to locate and evaluate sources, often instantaneously via the Internet, and serve as valuable tools for further research and debate.

Finally, Lucent's World History titles present rousing good stories, featuring vivid primary source quotations drawn from unique, sometimes obscure sources such as diaries, public records, and contemporary chronicles. In this way, the voices of participants and witnesses as well as important biographers and historians bring the study of history to life. As we are caught up in the lives of others, we are reminded that we too are characters in the ongoing human saga, and we are better prepared for our own roles.

B.C. ca. 400,000–200,000
Stone Age humans first arrive in India.

ca. 2600–1700 or somewhat later
The Harappan civilization flourishes in the Indus Valley and beyond.

ca. 1500
Traditional date for the purported but likely mythical Aryan invasion of India.

ca. 1200
Approximate date for the semimythical Trojan War, in which an alliance of Greeks sacks the Anatolian trading city of Troy.

ca. 1000
Iron tools and weapons come into use in India.

B.C.	400,000	2500	1800	1300	500

ca. 2686
Beginning of Egypt's Old Kingdom, in which Egypt's largest pyramids are built.

ca. 1500–ca. 500
India's Vedic Age, in which sacred religious writings, including the Vedas, appear and the Hindu faith evolves.

753
Traditional date for the founding of Rome, in western Italy.

ca. 563
Traditional date for the birth of Prince Siddhartha Gautama, who becomes known as the Buddha, or "Enlightened One."

ca. 1600
In Mesopotamia the city of Babylon is sacked by the Hittites, an ambitious people from Anatolia (what is now Turkey).

Time of Ancient India

ca. 543–491
Reign of King Bimbisara, who makes Magadha the most powerful and influential kingdom in India.

232
Death of Aśoka, under whom the Mauryan Empire reaches its greatest extent.

A.D. 79
The eruption of Mount Vesuvius, a volcano in western Italy, buries the Roman town of Pompeii, destroying but also preserving it.

476
As Europe is overrun by "barbarian" invasions and folk migrations, the last Roman emperor is forced from his throne.

400	300	100	A.D.100	200	500

326
The Macedonian Greek conqueror Alexander (later called "the Great") invades India.

146
Rome defeats the North African empire of Carthage in the last of the three Punic Wars.

ca. 320
Founding of the Gupta dynasty, associated with India's so-called cultural and intellectual "golden age."

321
Chandragupta Maurya establishes the Mauryan dynasty in Magadha.

ca. 480–530
The White Huns invade India and overrun the Gupta realm, ending the golden age.

A Nation In Touch with Its Past

As countries go, India is in no way average. With some 1.1 billion inhabitants, for example, it is second only to China in population. (But India is the world's most populous democracy.) India is also huge geographically speaking. The seventh largest nation on Earth, it covers 1,222,559 square miles (3,166,414 sq. km); it is so big, in fact, and has such a wide variety of terrains and climates, that it is often referred to as the Indian "subcontinent." In addition, India boasts the world's fourth largest economy; and its people belong to an unusual diversity of religious faiths, among them, Hinduism, Buddhism, Jainism, Islam, Christianity, Sikhism, Judaism, and Zoroastrianism.

A Cradle of Civilization

India is also remarkable from a historical standpoint. First, it nurtured one of the four advanced ancient cultures that modern historians refer to as the "cradles" of civilization. Each developed along the banks of a major river or rivers—the Tigris and Euphrates in Mesopotamia (what is now Iraq); the Nile in Egypt; the Huang in China; and the Indus in India. The first cities appeared in Mesopotamia in the mid-to-late fourth millennium (3000s) B.C.; and the world's first known nation-state was established in Egypt in about 3100 B.C.

But India was not far behind. By 3000-2600 B.C., what modern scholars call the Harappan civilization had begun to rise along the Indus and its tributaries. Some Harappan cities eventually grew to cover more than a square mile (2.6 sq. km) and supported populations of thirty to fifty thousand people. These city dwellers lived in thousands of sturdy brick houses lining well-planned streets laid out in modern-looking grid patterns. Moreover recent archaeological evidence from western India suggests that the Harappans carved out an empire larger than those

The Egyptian sun god Amun-Ra. The ancient Egyptians worshipped multiple gods and practiced numerous daily customs based on their faith.

of the Egyptians and Mesopotamians in the same era.

Preserving Ancient Cultures

Another way that India and its people are unusual, historically speaking, is the degree to which they maintain a continuity with their own distant past. Many modern Indians are far more in touch with the country's ancient cultures than the inhabitants of modern Mesopotamia and Egypt are with their own ancient roots. Today's Iraqis have almost nothing in common with the Mesopotamian peoples who built the first cities, for example. Indeed for the most part the religious, political, and social ideas of the Sumerians and Babylonians who inhabited early Mesopotamia are dead relics. Later peoples, including Arab Muslims, either conquered and eradicated the earlier ones or absorbed and converted them to their ways.

The same is true in Egypt. The ancient Egyptians worshipped multiple gods and practiced numerous daily customs based on their faith. Over time many foreign groups, including Persians, Greeks, Arab Muslims, and Turks, invaded and/or occupied Egypt. This process hastened the disappearance of ancient Egyptian culture; and almost all modern Egyptians are now monotheistic Muslims with radically different world views and religious customs.

In contrast a very different situation developed in India. There large numbers of people long perpetuated, and today continue to keep alive, many ideas and customs from ancient Indian cultures.

A majority of Indians "still worship the same gods," historian Sinharaja Tammita-Delgoda points out. "And they still chant the same verses and hymns which they recited 4,000 years ago."[1] Another scholar who has written extensively about ancient India—Alain Danielou—agrees. Because of "the continuity of its civilization," he says,

> India is itself a sort of history museum, with its separate departments preserving the cultures, races, languages, and religions that have come into contact over its vast territory, without ever mixing together or destroying each other. No invader has ever entirely eliminated the cultures of the more ancient peoples, and new beliefs and knowledge have never supplanted the beliefs and knowledge of former times.[2]

A Society with Many Faces

As a result of this extraordinary degree of cultural preservation and continuity, India does not possess a single, homogenous, monolithic culture. Rather the country features an amazing amount of cultural diversity and layering. As Delgoda puts it:

> The sheer wealth of Indian culture, its vast range and often dazzling color, has fascinated generation after generation of visitors. At the same time, they have often been bewildered by its infinite variety and complexity, its strangeness and its often horrifying

A Harappa mother-goddess statue, from the Indus Valley civilization, c. 2500–1500 B.C. After the passing of the Harappa civilization, new religious and social ideas were introduced into India.

contrasts. Over the course of time it has come to accommodate many different peoples, each with its own customs and traditions, and all of them speaking their own languages. The result is a society with several different faces, composed of layer upon layer of varied social groups.[3]

A number of those groups arrived in medieval and modern times. But some of them date back to India's ancient era. After the passing of Harappan civilization, new religious and social ideas were introduced; later Persians and Greeks invaded; and later still, a dizzying array of native kingdoms and empires, each with a rich culture, rose and fell. All of these left behind tangible traces of themselves, helping to make India the complex and diverse place it is today.

Chapter One

India's Earliest Inhabitants

India is a very ancient country in the sense that people lived there at an early stage of the long human saga. From the start the country's peculiar geography helped to determine how the earliest inhabitants entered the region and where they initially settled. Seen from far above, the Indian subcontinent forms an enormous triangle that is wide in the north and narrow in the south. The triangle measures some 2,000 miles (3,220km) from north to south and the same distance from west to east at its widest extent.

Within this huge territory there is a diverse mix of terrains and climates. Across India's northern border stretches the world's highest mountain range—the snow-capped Himalayas. These peaks, along with those of the Arakan range in the northeast, created a long barrier that kept migrants from central Asia from moving southward into India. Mountains, including the Hindu Kush range, are also

found in the northwest. However, several passes that meander through these peaks allowed ancient peoples to enter the subcontinent from a westerly direction.

Those who entered India this way found an enormous plain and river valley stretching southward from the foothills of the northern mountain ranges. Encompassing hundreds of thousands of square miles, this region is dominated by three major rivers—the Indus, the Ganges, and the Brahmaputra—along with their tributaries.

Large portions of this north-central region of India have been lush and fertile at various times in the last few thousand years. So it is not surprising that the earliest humans who entered the subcontinent settled there first. Over time they, and later arrivals, spread southward, where they encountered another highland zone consisting of the Vindhyas and Satpura ranges. These mountains, which are considerably smaller than the

Himalayas, lead to a vast southern plateau—the Deccan (which modern Indians most commonly call simply "the south"). The Deccan formed during gigantic volcanic eruptions that occurred millions of years ago, long before humans existed. Although the plateau is mostly rugged and arid, it is rimmed by coastal plains that enjoy considerably more rainfall and in some areas near tropical conditions.

Immigrants from the West

Exactly when early humans first entered India and inhabited the river valleys, the Deccan, and the coastal plains is unclear. Archaeologists think that the first waves of immigrants came from the west—from what are now Afghanistan and Iran— sometime between 400,000 and 200,000 years ago. They were primitive hunter-gatherers who led largely a nomadic existence as they followed migrating animal herds.

No physical remains of these people have yet been found. Evidence of their culture consists of a number of tools they made by fracturing pieces of soft stone to produce flakes having sharp edges. They used these tools to slice through and cut up animal hides. Flaked stone tools of this type have been found in many parts of India, including the Deccan. But they

The Mysterious Harappan Script

The people of the Indus Valley civilization possessed a script, or form of writing. It consists of about four hundred characters, mostly little pictograms (drawings or symbols that stand for ideas, objects, or words). The pictograms are most often arranged in small groups of three to ten, but never more than twenty; these groups may represent individual concepts or words or expressions. But there is no way to know for sure. This is because scholars have so far been unable to decipher the script, which bears no resemblance to any known language, says historian Sinharaja Tammita-Delgoda:

The most frustrating factor is the total lack of any kind of public inscriptions, such as a business document, a historical record, or a literary composition, which would serve to provide a parallel source of reference. Until a bilingual inscription is found and the script is eventually read by this means, it seems unlikely that we will be able to learn very much about the life and thought of the Indus people.

Sinharaja Tammita-Delgoda, *A Traveller's History of India*. New York: Interlink, 2003, p. 26.

are most numerous in the Punjab, the fertile northwestern region in which several rivers flow into the Indus. (The Punjab now straddles the border with Pakistan, which separated from India and became a new country in the 1940s. Also, most of the Indus River system, for millennia part of India, is now in Pakistan.)

Some more permanent settlements began to appear in India between 7000 and 6000 B.C. But their remnants are meager and little is known about those who lived in them. It was not until about 4000 B.C., or slightly later, that more substantial Neolithic communities arose. Archaeologists define Neolithic cultures as those

The world's highest mountain range, the Himalayas, stretches across the northern part of India.

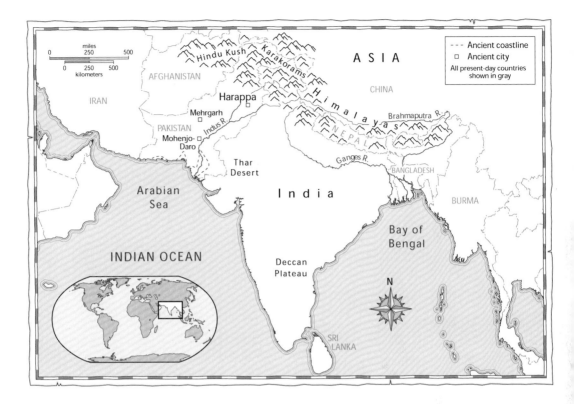

that practiced agriculture but continued to use stone tools and weapons. These settlements seem to have started in the northwest, in Baluchistan, now in southwestern Pakistan. The villagers "built houses of mud-brick, made their own pottery, and used stone and bone implements," Sinharaja Tammita-Delgoda explains.

They also bred their own livestock and raised sheep, goats, and cattle. There appear to have been several village communities in the region From about 3000 B.C. [on], similar settlements began to appear in many parts of the subcontinent, especially in the area around the Indus River Valley.[4]

The First Asian Empire?

Although the exact process is still uncertain, experts believe that these early agricultural communities steadily evolved into India's first major civilization. They call its builders the Harappans, after one of its chief cities, Harappa. Harappan culture is also frequently referred to as the Indus Valley civilization. No one knew that it had existed until 1856 (when India was a British colony). In that year British engineers John and William Brunton searched for track ballast (for a new railway) near the town of Harappa, on the left bank of the Ravi River in the Punjab. They found masses of fired bricks and used some of them for their railway project. They also notified Alexander Cunningham, an amateur Brit-

A Harappa archaeological site in India. The Harappa, or Indus Valley civilization, is considered by experts to be India's first major civilization.

ish archaeologist, who came and inspected the site. He found a number of ancient artifacts, along with some carved scripts that he could not read. After some brief, superficial excavations, Cunningham abandoned the site.

After that ancient Harappa was largely forgotten until 1921. It was then that large-scale, systematic digging began there under the direction of India's chief archaeologist, Sir John Marshall. It became clear that the ancient city had been erected circa 2600 B.C., which meant that India had supported an advanced culture far earlier than anyone had previously suspected. Not long afterward some of Marshall's assistants discovered an even larger Harappan city at Mohenjo

Daro (meaning "Mound of the Dead"), on the right bank of the Indus River, about 400 miles (644km) south of Harappa. They found that the buildings of Mohenjo Daro also dated to about 2600 B.C.

Over the years that followed, many hundreds of other Harappan cities, towns, and villages were discovered, and more than seventy are presently under excavation. These sites are scattered over an immense area of some 1.5 million square miles (3.9 million sq. km). This is larger than all of Pakistan and twice the size of the region controlled by imperial Egypt in the era in which the Harappans reached their height.

Moreover all of the Harappan sites are extremely similar in layout, in building materials, and in the still undeciphered script originally found at Harappa. "Our overwhelming impression," wrote two twentieth-century experts on the Indus Valley civilization, "is of cultural uniformity, both throughout the several centuries during which the Harappan civilization flourished, and over the vast area it occupied."[5] The natural inclination, therefore, is to see the sprawling collection of Harappan towns as either a large nation-state or an empire. If the latter is true, it was the first empire in Asia and indeed in the world. (The first Mesopotamian empire—the Akkadian—did not arise until about 2300 B.C.) However, scholars are still unsure about this hypothesis. Many think that the far-flung Harappan settlements may have been linked mainly by shared culture and that

The Great Bath at Mohenjo Daro

One of the largest buildings in Mohenjo Daro was what archaeologists think was a public bathhouse. It consisted of a rectangular hall lined with columns. In the center of the hall was a recessed pool similar in many ways to the municipal pools found in many modern U.S. towns and cities. The Harappan version was carefully sealed with bitumen (a tar-like substance) to make it water-tight and featured steps leading downward at each end. That people immersed themselves in this pool is certain. But why they did so remains unclear. It is possible that the pool was used for recreation, with ordinary citizens refreshing themselves or relaxing in the water, as in the ancient Roman baths. However, a number of scholars say the Harappan bath may instead have been used for religious purposes. If so, selected individuals immersed themselves as part of some sort of sacred ritual.

Harappan Weights and Measures

Archaeological evidence suggests that the Harappans had a well-developed merchant and artisan class, with individual, specialized professions such as trader, potter, brick-maker, metalsmith, and so on. These workers utilized a standardized system of weights and measures different from the systems used in ancient Mesopotamia, Egypt, and Greece. The basic unit in the Harappan system was a small cube of chert, a flint-like rock. Evidently merchants and artisans sold their wares by weight, corresponding to multiples of the basic unit. There were two scales of multiples—a small one and a big one. In the small scale, the multiples were based on doubling (i.e., 1, 2 (2 X 1), 4 (2 X 2), 8 (2 X 4), and so forth up to 64 units). The larger scale began with 160 units and employed multiples of 10, hence: 160 (16 X 10), 320 (16 X 20), 640 (16 X 40) and so forth. These standards prevailed in every Harappan settlement excavated to date.

they may have had their own local rulers. University of Cambridge scholar Gordon Johnson says:

> Mohenjo-Daro, the largest of the Indus Valley sites, does not appear to have exercised imperial power over the rest, though it probably formed some sort of administrative center. . . . Most archaeologists would argue that the [Harappan settlements] resembled a lose federation of peoples rather than a unified state.[6]

Well-planned, Uniform Cities

More certain is that the Harappans were highly skilled, well-organized, and prolific builders. Each of their larger cities was as big as or bigger than the chief Meso-potamian cities of the same era. Harappa, for example, was at least 3 miles (4.8km) in circumference and supported a population of 35,000 to 40,000 or more people.

Harappa and the other Indus Valley cities and towns also featured streets laid out in well-planned grid patterns, perhaps the first such neatly planned communities in the world. The roads in these grids are remarkably standardized and uniform. All run either north-to-south or east-to-west and converge at almost perfect right angles. In addition the main boulevards are either twice or one-and-a-half times as wide as the regular streets; and the streets are almost exactly twice as wide as the side-lanes and alleyways.

Lining these roads of varying widths are thousands of brick houses. Probably brick was used because stone suitable for building was, and remains, scarce in that region of India. The bricks were made by pressing wet clay into wooden molds, removing the moist bricks, and either letting them dry in the sun or firing them in kilns. Not only are Harappan bricks the same standard size across the vast Indus Valley, they are extremely similar to modern bricks. For this reason the first excavators at Mohenjo Daro initially thought the structures they were unearthing were less than a century old.

The Harappan houses vary in size, probably according to the wealth of the those who lived in them. Some are small with only two or three rooms; others are larger, with several rooms clustered around a central courtyard; still others are clearly mansions, with multiple courtyards and dozens of rooms. Though only sections of the ground floors now remain, many of these houses were originally two or three stories tall. Most had paved floors, a raised brick hearth for cooking, and bathrooms with carefully-planned drainage systems, as described by Delgoda:

The bath was taken, as it still is in many parts of India, by pouring water over the body from a large jar. Pottery drainpipes ran along the floor, taking the dirty water out into the street drains, which then flowed into sewers under the main streets. . . . It is an elaborate and extremely efficient system which has no parallel anywhere else in the ancient world.[7]

As for larger buildings, very few have been found in the Harappan ruins, which archaeologists find curious. Harappa

Two stone seals depicting animals were found during the excavation of Mahenjo Daro, an Indus Valley city.

and Mohenjo Daro do have large brick citadels, in each case erected on the western side of the city. These may have had defensive-military purposes, but a number of archaeologists remain uncertain. There are also some moderately large structures that seem to have been used to store grain. But no monumental (large-scale) buildings conclusively identified as temples or palaces have been found. One large structure, measuring 230 by 78 feet (70 by 23m), unearthed at Mohenjo Daro might be a palace. Yet it might instead be a mansion belonging to the richest family in the community. Scholar John Keay suggests that the lack of monumental Harappan structures may be due to the limitations of available building materials:

> Bricks, unlike dressed stone, must be kept small for good firing and are therefore less suitable for towering elevations and long-lasting monuments. Sun, salt, and wind play havoc with a mortar [made] of mud [and] weight stresses cause bowing and buckling. . . . Even supposing the Harappans had aspired to the monumental extravagances of their Egyptian contemporaries [i.e., huge temples, palaces, and pyramid-tombs], it is hard to see how they could have achieved them.[8]

The Harappans and the Larger World

With a civilization so extensive and culturally advanced, it is unlikely that the people of the Indus Valley could have remained completely isolated from and unknown to the other great civilizations of the time. And indeed they were far from isolated. The Sumerians and other peoples of Mesopotamia, though situated some 1,300 miles (2,092km) from the Indus Valley, were well aware of the existence of the Harappans. In fact the two civilizations carried on a moderately active trade for several centuries. Some scholars think that the term Meluhha, found in several Mesopotamian documents, may be the Sumerian word for the Harappans.

During the mature phase of the Indus Valley culture, lasting from about 2600 to 1900 B.C., small wooden Harappan merchant ships sailed down the Indus and into the Indian Ocean. From there they made their way northwestward and passed through what is now the Strait of Hormuz into the Persian Gulf. Several Sumerian cities then existed on or near the gulf's northwestern shores. The locals traded their own goods for Harappan grain; semiprecious stones, including lapis lazuli; and cotton cloth. In fact the Harappans appear to have been the first people in the world to spin cotton yarn into cloth. "This discovery ranks among India's greatest gifts to the world,"[9] Delgoda remarks.

Part of the evidence for this centuries-long trade connection between India and Mesopotamia takes the form of

The remains of an ancient city discovered in Lothal, India, in 1945. The city dates from 2400 to 1900 B.C.

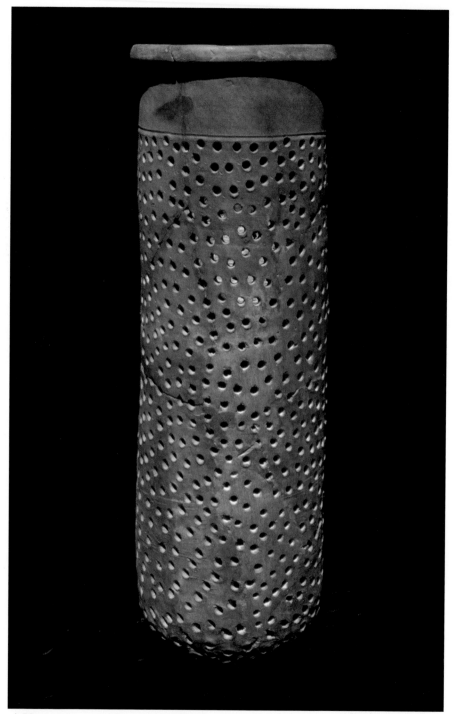

A Harappan ceramic pot. Artifacts such as this are all that remain of the Indus Valley civilization that began to decline around 1900 B.C.

seals, small disks made of terra-cotta (baked clay). These had pictures of animals, people, gods, or objects carved or stamped into them. Some were pressed into wet clay or liquid wax, leaving an impression that sealed a commercial deal or identified a merchant or other person or his family. It is possible that the Harappans also used seals as a form of currency, though that idea is still debated. More than two thousand Harappan seals have been found, most in the Indus region. But several have also been recovered from the ruins of Mesopotamian cities, attesting to trade between the two civilizations.

This long-distance trading network, coupled with the large number of extensive, well-built Harappan sites, is telling. The combination of these factors indicates that the Indus Valley culture long enjoyed considerable wealth, prosperity, and overall success. As Delgoda points out:

The sheer size and scale of the ruins suggest enormous wealth and a great deal of all-around prosperity. This was a society which could even afford to provide for the needs of its poorest and most lowly elements, even the workers or slaves. In many cases, they were far better housed than the average Indian laborer is today. The prosperity of this world rested on its stability; order was far more important than change.[10]

Decline and Fall

The Harappans' stability and prosperity, along with their commercial links to Mes-

opotamia, eventually diminished, however. The main reason seems to be that Harappan civilization went into steady decline beginning about 1900 B.C. (Historians sometimes refer to the era lasting from circa 1900 B.C. to circa 1300 B.C. as the Late Harappan period.) As buildings fell into disrepair, as they naturally do, fewer and fewer were repaired; and newer structures were smaller and poorly built. By 1700 B.C. or somewhat later, the larger Indus Valley settlements had been abandoned, except for a few impoverished squatters who lingered in the ruins for a few generations. Finally most of the Harappan sites became completely deserted and disappeared from view.

When these towns began to see the light of day again in the early 1900s, archaeologists and other scholars naturally wondered why the Harappans had declined and disappeared. At first some scattered shreds of evidence made some experts suspect that foul play had been involved; and a theory emerged that quickly became widely accepted. It proposed that the Indus Valley people were conquered and eradicated by a great wave of foreign invaders. Who were these intruders? Where did they come from? And why did they destroy the prosperous and apparently peace-loving Harappans? The effort to answer these questions became central to historical studies of India in the twentieth century and sparked heated debates that are still ongoing.

Chapter Two

The Aryans and the Vedic Age

Modern scholars call the historical period following the end of the Indus Valley civilization the Vedic Age. The term "Vedic" comes from the Vedas, a collection of verses written in an early form of Sanskrit, an Indian language that appeared in the subcontinent sometime in the early second millennium B.C. These verses, mostly taking the form of sacred hymns, prayers, and religious instructions, are attributed to a people that experts long called (and sometimes still call) the Aryans.

Throughout most of the twentieth century, archaeologists, historians, and those who read their books and articles saw the Aryans as, in a sense, the cornerstone of Indian history and culture. According to this view, this rustic but noble foreign race swept into India, initiating the Vedic Age. Experts differ somewhat on dates for the period; but the most common estimate is about 1500 B.C. to circa 500 B.C. Not only did the invaders destroy the Harappan cities and towns, the theory proposed, they also established the basic religious and social ideas and customs on which later Indian cultures were based.

Today, however, the terms "Aryans" and "Aryan civilization" are increasingly seen as both misnomers and outmoded. And terms such as "Vedic people" and "Vedic culture" are fast replacing them in history books. This is because of both the discovery of new evidence and reinterpretations of old evidence during the past two decades, a rising tide of information and opinion that has called the Aryan invasion hypothesis into question. Many scholars who specialize in Indian history now refer to it as the "Aryan myth." They agree with noted Indian archaeologist B.B. Lal when he says that the Aryan invasion and extinction of the Harappans "are nothing more than mere myths which, once created, have subconsciously been perpetuated. Since these have colored our vision of India's past, the sooner

[they] are cast away the better."[11] Because a few experts still support the theory, it remains a controversial and touchy subject in some scholarly circles.

The Aryan Hypothesis

How did this so-called myth originate? And why did so many experts adhere to it for so long? First, the notion that outsiders invaded India was partly based on a larger theory that became popular in the early 1800s. In the dim past, it proposed, nomadic, warlike, light-skinned peoples migrated in waves from south-central Asia into Europe, Mesopotamia, Iran, and India. Scholars at first referred to these ancient migrants as Indo-Europeans; but the terms Indo-Aryans and more simply Aryans soon gained equal usage. The idea of a large-scale invasion of India also seemed to be supported by the Vedic texts themselves. Sections of these writings describe a war between the powers of lightness and darkness. Most scholars of that time interpreted this not as a mythic battle between good and evil, but as a real war between dark-skinned natives and light-skinned invaders.

This theory was highly attractive to the British when they took control of India in the mid-1800s. The white-skinned, manly Aryans had "created" Indian civilization,

Seventeenth-century painting depicting a scene from the Bhagavata Purana, *writings thought to encompass all Vedic philosophy and literature.*

The Aryans and the Vedic Age ■ 27

The Vedic god Indra is referred to as the "destroyer of forts" in the Vedas. This depiction of Indra led some scholars to the belief that the Harappans were actually conquered by the Aryans.

Aryans, [bringing] a superior civilization and a humane religion, and ushering in a new golden age.[12]

Attempts to date this proposed Aryan invasion began in the 1850s when a noted German scholar of Sanskrit, Friedrich Max Muller, tried to date the Vedas. He suggested they had been written in about 1200 B.C. This was only a rough estimate based on the very limited evidence he had to work with at the time. He himself later admitted, "Whether the Vedic hymns were composed in 1000 or 1500 or 2000 or 3000 B.C., no power on earth will ever determine."[13]

Muller and others also proposed that the Aryans had entered India in about 1500 B.C. This date was highly speculative, as it was based on preconceived ideas about various biblical events rather than on hard evidence. A devout Christian, Muller thought that Noah's flood had wiped out most of humanity in about 2500 B.C. After that disaster, he reasoned, the Aryans required time to develop and multiply as a people and to migrate through Asia; therefore, they could not have reached India before 1500 B.C.

These dates, which turned out to be questionable at best, became firmly

the story went; but over many centuries their race had become diluted and degraded by "darker" peoples. "Then, in the nick of time," as John Keay puts it, out of the West came the British. No less fair, no less manly, and no less confident of their superiority, they were the neo-

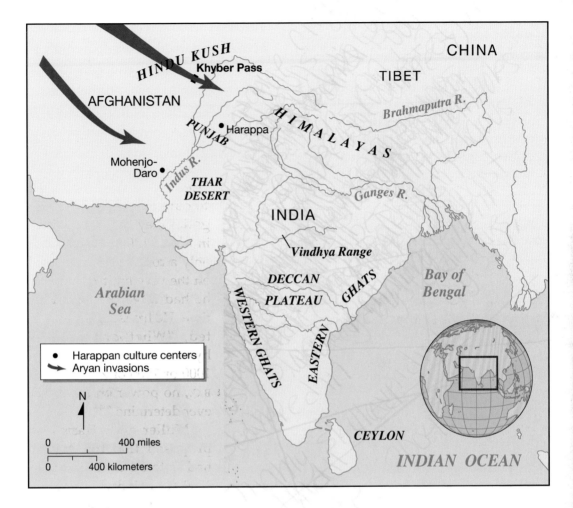

accepted by the scholarly community in the late nineteenth century. So when the Indus Valley civilization was discovered in the 1920s, experts immediately tried to fit it into the Aryan historical framework they had already constructed. First, evidence showed that the Harappans had flourished well before 1500 B.C. So, experts assumed, they could not be related to the Aryans, who did not arrive until that time. The fact that most of the Harappan cities were abandoned in the early second millennium B.C. also seemed to fit the Aryan invasion scenario. Simply put, most scholars jumped to the conclusion that the foreign Aryans had overrun what was left of a rapidly declining native culture.

This idea gained even more credence in the 1940s when British archaeologist Mortimer Wheeler found a fortification wall at Harappa. Because one of the Vedic gods—Indra—is referred to as a "destroyer of forts"[14] in one of the Vedas, Wheeler saw it as more evidence of the Aryan conquest of the Harappans. In short, at the mid-point of the twentieth century the vast majority of scholars accepted the dramatic scenario summarized here by Keay. "The Aryan nomads," he says:

. . . hurtled down the passes from Afghanistan [and onto] the plains of the Punjab. Dealing death and destruction from fleets of horse-drawn chariots, they subdued the indigenous peoples and [stole] their herds. [These natives] were characterized as dark, flat-nosed, uncouth, incomprehensible, and generally inferior. The Aryans, on the other hand, were finer-featured, fairer, taller, favored above others in the excellence of their gods . . . and altogether a very superior people.[15]

Remains of a granary in Harappa, Pakistan. The overuse of land for farming and a fall in trade were probably the two reasons for the destruction of the Harappan people.

Objections to the Invasion Theory

As time went on, however, an increasing number of archaeologists and other experts began to suspect that the invasion theory's foundations were shaky. First, new evidence about the Harappans' demise came to light in the late twentieth century. It showed that, while the Indus Valley culture as a whole declined over time, pockets of it survived well into the late second millennium B.C. In fact several new Harappan settlements were built during these years in the outer fringes of the Indus Valley. This seemed to indicate a migration away from the central part of the valley. Also, increasing evidence indicated that the abandonment of large sectors of that central region had not been caused by violence. According to one of Mohenjo Daro's chief excavators during the 1970s:

> There is no destruction level covering the latest period of the city, no sign of extensive burning, no bodies of warriors clad in armor and surrounded by the weapons of war. [And] the citadel, the only fortified part of the city, yielded no evidence of a final defense.[16]

Instead more and more evidence pointed to major climatic, environmental, and economic changes as the main causes of the Harappans' demise. Scholars found that large portions of the central Indus Valley became unusually arid in the early second millennium B.C., which must have seriously damaged agriculture in the region. Agricultural output also declined, Lal points out, because of "over-exploitation and consequent wearing out of the landscape." In addition, "a marked fall in trade, both internal as well as external," dealt a huge blow to the Harappans' economy and standard of living. "As a result of all this, there was no longer the affluence that used to characterize this civilization. The cities began to disappear and there was a reversion to a rural scenario."[17]

What is more, one of the major rivers in western India—the Sarasvati, on whose banks many Harappan towns existed—completely dried up in this same period. On the one hand, this would explain why some Harappans migrated away toward the east and west and erected new towns. On the other, it raises an important objection to the traditional dating of the Aryans' appearance in India. The Vedas frequently refer to the Sarasvati as a wide, flowing river and to major Aryan settlements built along its banks. "The Sarasvati River went dry at the end of the Indus Valley culture and before the so-called Aryan invasion [in] 1500 B.C.," writes David Frawley, an expert on Vedic culture. "How could the Vedic Aryans know of this river and establish their culture on its banks if it dried up before they arrived?"[18] The answer, of course, is that the Aryans could not have known about and lived beside the Sarasvati if they had arrived in 1500 B.C. This means that they were already in western India at least as early as 2000 B.C. and likely considerably earlier.

But no matter *when* the Aryans arrived, the traditional theory holds that they were foreigners, with different geo-

Invoking the War God

The oldest of the Vedas, the Rig-Veda, contains numerous hymns to the Vedic deities, including several dedicated to Indra, god of war and the weather. This hymn calls upon Indra to help his worshipers achieve victory in battle.

Indra, bring wealth that gives delight, the victor's ever-conquering wealth, most excellent, to be our aid. By means of which we may repel our foes in battle hand to hand, by you assisted with the chariot. Aided by you, the thunder-armed, Indra, may we lift up the spear, and conquer all our foes in [the] fight. With you, O Indra, [as our] ally with missile-darting heroes, may we conquer our embattled foes. Mighty is Indra, yes, [he is] supreme; greatness be his, the Thunderer. Wide as the heaven extends his power, which aids those to win them sons, who come as heroes to the fight. . . . So also is his excellence, great, vigorous, rich in cattle, like a ripe branch to the worshiper.

Rig-Veda, Book 1, Hymn 8, trans. Ralph T.H. Griffith. http://www.sacred-texts.com/hin/rigveda/rv01008.htm

---

graphical origins and racial traits. If so there ought to be measurable differences in physical and genetic make-up between them and the indigenous Harappans. To test this supposition, forensic studies of some three hundred Harappan skeletons were conducted in 1984 and 1991. These found no significant changes in the physical characteristics of peoples living in the region either during or immediately following the decline of the Indus Valley culture. In fact, the studies showed that for the most part the Harappans closely resembled most modern Indians.

What is more, a 1994 examination of ancient and modern Indian DNA samples yielded similar results. The experts who conducted the study knew that, if the Aryans were indeed a separate group from outside the country, significant changes should have occurred in the DNA makeup of the inhabitants when the Aryans conquered and replaced the native Harappans. Yet the study indicated no significant genetic or racial differences between the Harappans and modern Indians. There was instead a remarkable physical continuity among Indians over the centuries.

Alternative Scenarios

These and other archaeological and forensic studies and discoveries opened the eyes of many scholars. The new evidence seemed to indicate that no large-scale migration and/or invasion of Aryans, or any other foreign group, occurred during the Harappan era or in the centuries immediately following it. Rather, it seemed that Vedic culture had developed out of, rather than destroyed and replaced, Harappan civilization. This realization has prompted a number of new theories about India's inhabitants in the third and second millennia B.C.

In one of these alternate scenarios, small groups of foreign migrants entered western India a little at a time over the course of many centuries. As they did so, their culture combined with, or was absorbed into, that of the existing Harappans. Eventually economic, political, and social changes, perhaps in large part stimulated by long-term climatic and ecological problems, brought about the rise of Vedic culture.

Another hypothesis that many scholars see as more compelling proposes that the Harappans absorbed foreign ideas rather than the outsiders themselves. In this sce-

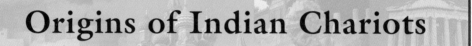

Origins of Indian Chariots

Chariots are mentioned often in the Vedas. For a long time scholars thought that the Aryans introduced the spoked wheel and the chariot to India during their supposed invasion in the mid-second millennium B.C. However, more recent evidence shows that the Harappans used spoked wheels well before that time. So they may have had chariots, too, an idea they may have either borrowed from Mesopotamia or developed on their own. Or the native Indians may have begun using chariots later, as they entered their "Vedic" phase. Another argument against the notion of Aryan nomads invading with chariots comes from scholar David Frawley:

The whole idea of nomads with chariots has been challenged. Chariots are not the vehicles of nomads. Their usage occurred only in ancient urban cultures with much flat land, of which the river plain of north India was the most suitable. Chariots are totally unsuitable for crossing mountains and deserts, as the so-called Aryan invasion required.

David Frawley, "The Myth of the Aryan Invasion of India." http://www.hindunet.org/hindu_history/ancient/aryan/aryan_frawley.html

Krishna and Arjuna leaving for battle in a scene from the Mahabharata, *one of India's great epic poems.*

nario a few outsiders migrated into western India in the early second millennium B.C. (or perhaps earlier). And for reasons now unclear, they exerted an unusually strong cultural influence on the existing natives. In other words, the late Harappans may have borrowed various religious, social, and technological elements they saw as useful or attractive from a few influential immigrants. But the latter left no noticeable traces of themselves in the archaeological and genetic records. Over time these borrowed cultural elements wrought so much change that the natives developed a new culture—the Vedic. "The process appears simply to have been one of gradual [cultural assimilation]," Keay says, "requiring neither mass migration

nor [conquest]."[19] This theory stresses the continuity of indigenous Indian civilization, a quality seen among the Harappans during their prime and among all the Indian cultures that followed them.

Vedic Sacred Texts

In whatever manner the Vedic people came to inhabit western India, they eventually spread into the Ganges River valley and further eastward and southward into the subcontinent. Very little of a concrete nature is known about their personal lives, habits, and customs. This is mostly because, unlike their Harappan forebears, they were not highly urbanized; so they did not leave behind extensive ruins containing artifacts of daily life. Instead the

Vedic people, at least during the initial centuries of the Vedic Age, were mainly rural, agrarian folk who raised cattle and sheep and grew a few crops. They lived on farms and in small villages, which were flimsy and impermanent and left few traces in the archaeological record.

The Vedic people did, however, leave behind several major literary works that describe some of their religious beliefs and myths and basic political and social structure. The first of these works, of course, were the Vedas. The oldest is the Rig-Veda (meaning "Rich in Knowledge"), organized into ten books, each containing many hymns to Vedic gods. Three other Vedas (the Sama-Veda, Yajur-Veda, and Atharva-Veda) were composed later.

Somewhat after 1000 B.C., religious leaders apparently felt the need to supplement the Vedic texts. So they produced the Brahmanas, which explain the rituals described in the Vedas, and the Upanishads, philosophical commentaries that discuss and interpret the spiritual elements of the Vedic texts. Vedic culture also produced India's two great epic poems—the *Ramayana* and the *Mahabharata*. The former tells of the heroic deeds of Rama, a prince who is also an incarnation of the god Vishnu. The *Mahabharata*, a huge work of

DNA sample comparisons between ancient and modern Indians showed that the Harappans' DNA makeup closely resembles that of modern Indian people.

74,000 verses, describes the struggle for a kingly throne within the larger context of divine will and universal fate.

All of these writings were at first preserved strictly through oral tradition—memorization and frequent recital by priests or special performers. Only later were they written down. The two epics, for example, did not appear in book form until about 500–400 B.C., actually after the end of the Vedic Age. The first written versions of the Vedas probably did not exist until considerably later.

Vedic Society

These writings reveal that the Vedic people, who were divided into various tribes, eventually developed small kingdoms, each inhabited by members of a tribe. The ruler of a kingdom was called a raja. A council of elders advised him on political and social policy and a high priest guided him in religious matters. Also aiding the raja was a military expert, probably the kingdom's chief army officer.

Meanwhile Vedic Indian society came to be divided into four social classes, the

Origins of the Caste System

One rationale often offered for the Indian caste system, which developed in the Vedic Age, is that its creation was described in a hymn in the sacred Rig-Veda. The subject of the hymn is Purusha (or Purusa), a primeval (very ancient) giant with thousands of heads, feet, and eyes. Supposedly the early gods dismembered his body and some of the parts became the varnas, or human castes.

A thousand heads has Purusha, a thousand eyes, a thousand feet. On every side pervading earth he fills a space ten fingers wide. This Purusha is all that yet has been and all that is to be. The Lord of Immortality . . . so mighty is his greatness. . . . All creatures are one-fourth of him, three-fourths eternal life in heaven. . . . When they [the gods] divided Purusha how many portions did they make? What do they call his mouth, his arms? What do they call his thighs and feet? The Brahmans [came from] his mouth, of both his arms were the Kshatriyas made. His thighs became the Vaishyas, [and] from his feet the Sudras were produced.

Rig-Veda, Book 10, Hymn 90, trans. by Ralph T.H. Griffith. http://www.sacred-texts.com/hin/rigveda/rv10090.htm

varnas. The smallest and most revered class was that of the Brahmins, priest-like individuals who knew and interpreted the Vedic texts and oversaw sacred rituals. Next came the warrior class—the Kshatriyas. Among its ranks were the rajas, their advisors, army officers, and other wealthy and influential people. The third class, the Vaishyas, contained merchants, traders, artisans, and other respectable workers. In the last, lowest, and likely most populous class—the Sudras—were serfs and other menial workers who more or less served those in the upper classes. These Vedic social classes formed the basis of the caste system that developed later in India.

Similarly the Vedic texts show that Vedic religious beliefs and practices were the basis for one of India's great religions—Hinduism, which developed in the second half of the Vedic Age. In fact, Hinduism is essentially a more complex and mature form of the Vedic faith; and many elements of the latter were retained in Hindu beliefs and rituals. The chief Vedic deity, Indra, is a prominent example. Originally the god of war and master of the weather, he remained in the Hindu pantheon (group of gods), though his status was now lower than that of some other deities.

Religion was not all that changed and evolved during the late Vedic Age. Sometime around 1000 B.C. iron tools and weapons began to supplant those of stone, copper, and bronze. Also, pastoralism (the raising of livestock), especially cattle-ranching, the economic mainstay of early Vedic society, became less important than growing crops. In addition the many, scattered Vedic tribal states steadily coalesced into fewer, larger, and stronger kingdoms. With the emergence of these kingdoms and the increasing rivalry between them, India entered a new age. It would witness a series of momentous events, among them attacks by foreign invaders and the rise of India's first empires.

Chapter Three

Invasions from the West

Modern scholars refer to the last few centuries of the Vedic Age (ca. 1000 B.C. to ca. 500 B.C.) in various ways depending on the context. The era is sometimes called India's Iron Age because it witnessed the spread of iron tools and weapons throughout the subcontinent. From a cultural and artistic viewpoint, late Vedic culture is often called the Painted Grey Ware Culture, in reference to the predominant form of pottery in India in those centuries.

Another way of looking at the late Vedic Age is as India's second period of urbanization. The first city-builders in the region, of course, had been the Harappans. Their descendants, the early Vedic people, had adopted a more rural, pastoral lifestyle. But as city-states and small kingdoms began to appear in northern India's river valleys during the Iron Age, some villages grew into towns and a few of the towns grew into small cities.

At the same time some of the local city-states and kingdoms grew larger, often by absorbing some of their neighbors. Magadha, a kingdom in northeastern India, for example, expanded in size and prominence by conquering some nearby independent states. By about 600 B.C., near the end of the Vedic Age, all of northern India and parts of the south were governed by sixteen moderate-to-large-sized kingdoms. Historians generally refer to them collectively as the Mahajanapadas, usually translated as "great kingdoms" or "great countries." Magadha eventually emerged as the strongest and most influential of these kingdoms.

These trends of urbanization and political centralization were among the factors that brought the Vedic Age to a close and ushered in a new era characterized by empire-building. Another major factor was the influence of foreign empires, which suddenly imposed themselves on

India. In the sixth century B.C., parts of the Indus Valley were invaded by the Persian Empire, centered in Iran. This sector of India actually became a Persian province. Then, only two centuries later, a Macedonian Greek king, Alexander III (later called "the Great"), conquered Persia. His military adventures led him into India, where he significantly altered the existing balance of power. Moreover, though he died soon afterward, Alexander left behind Greek governors, troops, merchants, and artisans. They and their descendants subsequently produced a hybrid, Greco-Indian, culture in the region that had a significant impact on Indian culture.

The Rise of Magadha

Fortunately for Magadha's inhabitants, their country was not negatively affected by the foreign invasions, as a number of other Indian kingdoms were. This was largely because Magadha was located in eastern India and had no direct contact with the intruders. In fact, politically and militarily speaking, Magadha actually benefited from the invasions. While the western Indian states were falling or making concessions to the Persians and Greeks, Magadha remained strong and vital.

Because of a lack of reliable evidence, Magadha's history before 600 B.C. is very sketchy. More certain is that by the early 540s B.C. it controlled most of the Ganges River valley and was the wealthiest and militarily the strongest of the Mahajanapadas. Moreover, the Magadhan rulers who followed remained ambitious. Sometime in the late 500s B.C. King Bimbisara (reigned ca. 543–491 B.C.) conquered the kingdom of Kashi, lying northwest of the Magadhan heartland; he also annexed the smaller kingdom of Anga, situated west of Magadha, just north of the Bay of Bengal.

A statue of Alexander the Great, whose adventures led him into India where he eventually changed the balance of power in the country.

Also aggressive was Bimbisara's son, King Ajatashatru (reigned ca. 491–461 B.C.), who made war on the powerful kingdom of Kosala, located northwest of Kashi. Another of Ajatashatru's achievements was to build a splendid new capital, carrying on the urbanizing trend begun in late Vedic times. Sometime in the 480s B.C., the old Magadhan capital of Rajagriha ("The King's House"), situated about 80 miles (129km) due south of the Ganges, lost its royal status to the new city of Pataliputra, on the river's northern bank.

It may have been during either Bimbisara's or Ajatashatru's reign that a new religion, Buddhism, emerged in the Ganges Valley. It coexisted with, rather than replaced, Hinduism, mainly because its philosophical concepts were compatible with many Hindu beliefs. Buddhism spread rapidly through the rest of the subcontinent and in time beyond, becoming India's chief cultural export.

Persian Penetration of India

While these events were transpiring in eastern India, parts of western India were undergoing political upheaval and cultural readjustment, the results of the Persian invasion. The Persian Empire had rather suddenly appeared in the mid-500s B.C. when Cyrus II, a local Iranian prince, had led a successful rebellion against the Medes, who then controlled most of Iran and Mesopotamia. Having taken charge

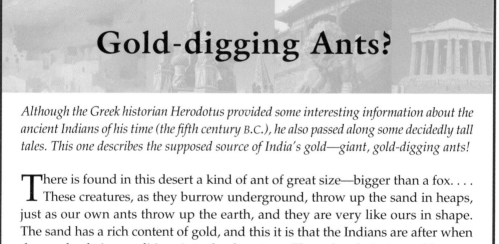

Gold-digging Ants?

Although the Greek historian Herodotus provided some interesting information about the ancient Indians of his time (the fifth century B.C.), he also passed along some decidedly tall tales. This one describes the supposed source of India's gold—giant, gold-digging ants!

There is found in this desert a kind of ant of great size—bigger than a fox. . . . These creatures, as they burrow underground, throw up the sand in heaps, just as our own ants throw up the earth, and they are very like ours in shape. The sand has a rich content of gold, and this it is that the Indians are after when they make their expeditions into the desert. . . . They plan their time-table so as actually to get their hands on the gold during the hottest part of the day, when the heat will have driven the ants underground. . . . When the Indians reach the place where the gold is, they fill their bags . . . and start for home again as fast as they can go, for the ants . . . smell them and at once give chase.

Ruins of the palace of Darius I in Persepolis, Iran. The exact details of Darius's invasion of India is not know, but he was able to establish a regular route to the Indian Ocean through the country.

of the lands within the Median realm, Cyrus initiated major military reforms and assembled a large army. During the next few years he invaded and annexed several foreign lands lying both west and east of his Iranian-Mesopotamian power base. Among the eastern regions he overran were Bactria (the ancient name for what is now northern Afghanistan) and at least parts of the Indian kingdom of Gandhara, in the northwestern Punjab.

A second and larger Persian invasion of India occurred during the reign of the third Persian king, Darius I, who came to power circa 522 B.C. According to the fifth-century B.C. Greek historian Herodotus, Darius first ordered scouts to explore sections of the Indus Valley. "He wanted to find out where the Indus joins the sea," Herodotus wrote. "And for this purpose [he] sent off on an expedition down the river a number of men whose word he could trust."[20] These explorers did reach the river's delta, and after a journey of more than two years they returned to Persia.

Darius then launched his invasion. Very little is known about the details, including exactly when it occurred and the amount of Indian territory seized.

Origins of Modern Terms Describing India

It was during the Persian occupation of parts of India's Punjab region that the roots of the modern western terms Indus, India, Hindu, and Hinduism were born. In Sanskrit the Punjab was called the Sapta-Sindhu, meaning "land of the seven rivers." In their own language, which was related to Sanskrit, the Persians replaced the initial "s" of Sanskrit words with an aspirate "h," which changed Sindhu to Hindhu, or Hindu. Later, when the Greeks adopted the word, they dropped the initial "h," rendering it as Indu, which became the root for the terms Indus and India. Meanwhile, however, Arabic-speaking peoples in western Asia retained both the "h" and the root word Hindu from the old Persian. So the Arabs came to call India Hindustan. And the term Hindu passed from Muslim lands into Europe as the name of the people of Hindustan. Finally, adding the suffix ism to Hindu produced Hinduism, the modern western term for India's main native religion.

Herodotus says only that "Darius subdued the Indians and [thereafter] made regular use of the southern [i.e., Indian] ocean."[21] As for when the invasion began, the best estimate of modern scholars is 516–515 B.C. They disagree on the extent of Darius's conquest. But it is probably safe to say that it included most of the Punjab lying west of the Indus. There is no firm evidence that the Persians ever controlled any Indian territory east of that river.

Whichever Indian lands did fall to the Persians, they became a satrapy, or province, of the Persian Empire. Herodotus mentions this province—called Gandhara, after the conquered Indian kingdom—as do other ancient historians. He says that it was the richest of Persia's twenty satrapies, supplying the king with gold and other valuables. Indian men who lived in the province also were expected to serve in the Persian army; and some of these Indian troops accompanied Darius's son Xerxes (ZERK-seez, reigned 486–465 B.C.) on his famous military expedition to Greece in 480 B.C. The Indian foot soldiers were "dressed in cotton," according to Herodotus. "They carried cane bows and cane arrows tipped with iron." There were also Indian fighters "on horseback" and "some in chariots drawn by either horses or wild asses."[22]

The Coming of Alexander

The Persians introduced a number of political ideas, religious customs, and Near Eastern languages into western India. But Persian influences in this region were mostly short-lived and ultimately overshadowed by Greek ones. This was partly because the Greek invasion of the subcontinent was more extensive and affected a larger number of western Indian kingdoms.

The rulers of these kingdoms had heard of Alexander's extraordinary military skills and exploits well before his arrival. They knew that he had brought the Persian realm, the largest empire in world history up to that time, to its knees. He had crossed into Asia in 334 B.C. and with amazing speed conquered the Persian territories of Anatolia (what is now Turkey), Syria, Palestine, Egypt, Mesopotamia, and Iran. Then he had moved eastward into Bactria. In 327 B.C. he was ready to push onward into the Indus Valley. Hearing these reports, Indian leaders were afraid and, as John Keay tells it, many of them decided it would be more prudent to give in to Alexander than to fight him:

Like a tidal wave, news of Alexander's prowess had swept ahead of him, flattening resistance and sucking him forward. Indian defectors from the Persian forces primed his interest and paved the way. Local [Indian rulers] promised support [and] sought his friendship.[23]

Having met little resistance, in the spring of 326 B.C. Alexander crossed the

A battle scene engraved on Alexander's sarcophagus, or coffin. Indian leaders thought it was better to give in to Alexander when he tried to conquer India than attempt to fight him.

Alexander III the Great (left) charges forward after lancing Porus in combat during the Battle of Hydaspes.

Indus and arrived at the city of Taxila. There he received a warm welcome from the local Indians. He also received presents and offers of alliance from ambassadors representing nearby Indian states.

The Battle of Hydaspes

One Indian ruler was not so quick to capitulate to the invaders, however. He was Porus (or Puru), raja of the kingdom of Pauravaa, located east of the Hydaspes River in the Punjab. (Hydaspes is the Greek name for the river; the ancient Indians called it the Vitasta and today it is goes by its Muslim name, the Jhelum.) Porus must have been a powerful ruler of a populous realm, for he was able to amass an army of thirty thousand infantry (foot soldiers), four thousand cavalry (horsemen), and two hundred war

elephants along the Hydaspes' eastern bank.

The Macedonians and other Greeks, reinforced by some five thousand Indian troops from Taxila, marched to the river. As Alexander's chief ancient biographer, the Greek Arrian, writes, they could "see Porus, with all of his forces, including his squadron of elephants, on the further side." A contest now ensued in which the Greeks tried to cross the river and Porus attempted to stop them. "Porus remained on guard in person," says Arrian, and sent units of soldiers

to the various other points along the river where a crossing was practicable, for he was determined to stop the Greeks from getting over. Alexander's answer was continual movement of his own troops to keep Porus guessing. . . . Every night [Alexander] kept moving the greater part of his troops up and down the bank of the river, making as much noise as possible.[24]

Porus ordered his troops to follow these mobile units of Greeks closely in case one of them suddenly attempted to ford the river. But despite these efforts, Alexander managed to find an unguarded spot along the riverbank several miles upstream from his main camp. There he led a contingent of his army across the Hydaspes. Hearing of this Porus hurried to check the enemy advance.

But even before the opposing armies clashed, the Indians were already at a disadvantage. Following a clever plan Alexander had devised, one of his generals, Craterus, now led the main body of the Greek army from its camp, across the river, and toward Porus's rear. Porus was "compelled to split [his] force into two," according to Arrian. This proved disastrous for the Indians. When Alexander's forces charged forward, Porus's men "fell back in confusion upon the elephants, their impregnable fortress, or so they

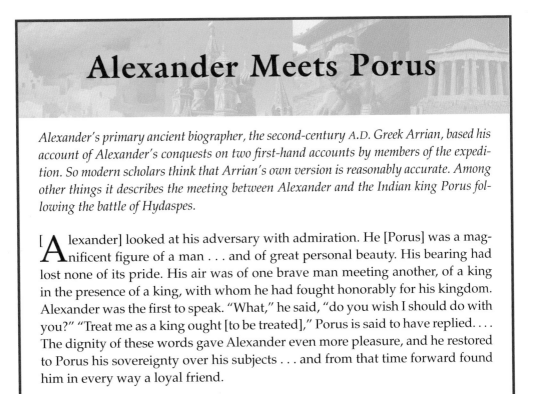

Alexander Meets Porus

Alexander's primary ancient biographer, the second-century A.D. Greek Arrian, based his account of Alexander's conquests on two first-hand accounts by members of the expedition. So modern scholars think that Arrian's own version is reasonably accurate. Among other things it describes the meeting between Alexander and the Indian king Porus following the battle of Hydaspes.

[Alexander] looked at his adversary with admiration. He [Porus] was a magnificent figure of a man . . . and of great personal beauty. His bearing had lost none of its pride. His air was of one brave man meeting another, of a king in the presence of a king, with whom he had fought honorably for his kingdom. Alexander was the first to speak. "What," he said, "do you wish I should do with you?" "Treat me as a king ought [to be treated]," Porus is said to have replied. . . . The dignity of these words gave Alexander even more pleasure, and he restored to Porus his sovereignty over his subjects . . . and from that time forward found him in every way a loyal friend.

Arrian, *Anabasis Alexandri,* published as *The Campaigns of Alexander.* Trans. Aubrey de Sélincourt. New York: Penguin, 1971, p. 281.

hoped."[25] This hope was soon dashed. Using showers of spears and arrows, the Greeks forced many of the huge beasts back into the Indian ranks, where they did a great deal of damage, and the rest of Porus's army retreated. The enormity of Porus's loss is clear from the casualty reports, as later reported by Arrian:

Nearly 20,000 of the Indian infantry were killed . . . and about 3,000 of their cavalry. All their war chariots were destroyed. Among the dead were two sons of Porus. . . . The surviving elephants were captured. Out of Alexander's original 6,000 infantry, some eighty were killed. In addition to these, he lost ten mounted archers and [about 220 of his] cavalry.[26]

Following the battle Porus, who had been wounded, met with Alexander. When the Macedonian king asked his defeated opponent how he wished to be treated, the proud and unafraid Porus answered, "As a king!"[27] Alexander was so impressed with Porus's courage and dignity that he restored him to his throne; of course implicit in the deal was the reality that Pauravaa was now a Greek ally that would do Alexander's bidding and supply him with troops and supplies.

The Greco-Indian Cultures

Indeed Alexander needed large amounts of supplies to support his troops in their continued eastward march. He planned to conquer the rest of India. But in particular he had set his sights on seizing the great east-Indian kingdom of Magadha, which

he had heard was rich and powerful. The problem was that rumors saying that Magadha had an army considerably bigger and more lethal than Porus's (which it did) spread through the Greek ranks. Alexander's men were already exhausted from years of marching and fighting far from home. The projected invasion of Magadha was, for them, the proverbial last straw. Upon reaching the Hyphasis River (now the Beas), they simply refused to march any further east.

Having no other choice Alexander agreed to turn back. He died in the Mesopotamian city of Babylon (at the age of thirty-three) less than three years later (323 B.C.). Most of the lands he had taken in the Punjab were overrun by the Magadhan army his men had been reluctant to face. However, Bactria and other nearby lands that Alexander had conquered remained in Greek hands. So in the years that followed many thousands of Greek farmers, merchants, artisans, and others settled in what are now northern Afghanistan and Pakistan.

At first these Greek-ruled areas owed allegiance to one of Alexander's successors, Seleucus I, who also ruled Mesopotamia and Iran. But as he and his own successors became embroiled in wars in the western part of their realm, their hold on Bactria weakened. In about 250 B.C. the Bactrian Greeks broke away from the Seleucid Empire and established the Greco-Bactrian kingdom. And that same pattern was repeated three generations later. In about 180 B.C., Demetrius, son of the Greco-Bactrian king Euthydemus I, invaded India. In only five years Deme-

A tetradrachma, or Greek coin, bearing the likeness of Seleucus I, ca. 300 B.C.

trius and his general, Menander, managed to conquer the entire Indus Valley and some Indian areas beyond it. Soon afterward they broke away from the Greco-Bactrian kingdom and established their own realm, the Indo-Greek kingdom. Menander, who succeeded Demetrius on the throne of this new state, proved to be the greatest of a series of Indo-Greek kings who ruled until about 10 B.C.

Greek cultural influences introduced into India in these centuries were considerable and long-lasting. They were part of a hybrid Greco-Indian culture in which ideas and customs flowed both ways between Greeks and Indians. Menander converted to Buddhism, for instance, as did many other Indo-Greeks. Similarly, Greek coinage styles spread across India and remained in use for many centuries. What is more a number of Greek words, including those for "book," "pen," "ink," and several military terms, permanently entered Sanskrit.

Particularly important were Greek artistic influences, which produced the hybrid Greco-Buddhist style of sculpture. Greeks and Indians either trained by or imitating Greeks created finely crafted busts and statues of Buddha; they showed him with wavy hair, draped cloaks, sandals, and carved decorations featuring acanthus leaves, all Greek artistic motifs. Although Buddha was a prophet rather than a god, Greek sculptors had a strong tradition of carved statues of gods. So the new style portrayed Buddha as a "man-god." This image of Buddhism's founder was subsequently adopted by other Asian peoples, including the Chinese and the inhabitants of faraway Japan.

From 326 to 10 B.C., therefore, Greeks ruled large portions of western India or nearby lands and created a lasting cultural heritage in the region. They were unable to penetrate other parts of the subcontinent, however, where native Indians held firm sway. Indeed a mere two years after Alexander's death, a new dynasty arose in Magadha. The members of this ruling family were destined to forge a realm that would dwarf all that had come before it in India.

Chapter Four

The Mauryan Empire

Because the Persian and Greek intrusions into India had little direct, immediate effect on the kingdoms of eastern India, Magadha was able to grow more powerful while many Indian states became weaker. Well before the foreign invasions, a dynasty of Magadhan rulers, the Nandas, had created a very large army. With this potent tool they had expanded their holdings and influence in the region.

The dynasty that followed in Magadha—the Mauryan—inherited that country's huge military establishment. Employing it and their own considerable political skills wisely, the Mauryans built on the foundations their predecessors had laid and achieved a level of success the Nandas had only dreamed about. The Mauryan Empire eventually encompassed almost the entire Indian subcontinent, an unprecedented accomplishment at the time. As Sinharaja Tammita-Delgoda points out:

No Indian dynasty before them had enjoyed so much power, and it is doubtful whether any regime since has been able to exercise such complete and effective control over so much of this vast country.[28]

The Nanda Dynasty

Magadha was already the most influential kingdom in eastern India at the time the Nandas came to power under their first and greatest ruler, Mahapadma Nanda. The date of the dynasty's inception is uncertain. This is partly because only a few ancient Indian sources from that era have survived. Also, most of these sources differ on the date in question, as well as on the years of Mahapadma's reign. At present some modern scholars estimate that he ascended the Magadhan throne circa 424 B.C. and ruled until about 362 B.C. Other experts favor an alternative "short chronology" for the Nanda period

This relief from a Buddhist stupa, or shrine, from the Mauryan period depicts the head of a man inside a lotus blossom. At one time, the Mauryan Empire encompassed the entire Indian subcontinent.

that places the start of his reign around 380 B.C.

Whenever he actually lived and ruled, Mahapadma Nanda is often called India's first historical emperor. He and his sons, and perhaps grandsons, who followed him were certainly the subcontinent's first would-be empire-builders. Very little of a personal nature is known about them, although some brief facts about Mahapadma appear in both ancient Indian and ancient western sources. For example, supposedly he was the first Indian king born of a low caste, presumably the Sudras. According to the first century A.D. Roman historian Curtius (Quintus Curtius Rufus), Mahapadma started out as

a barber whose regular employment barely kept starvation at bay, but by his good looks, he won the heart of the queen. By her, he had been [introduced to] the king of the time, whom he then treacherously murdered, seizing the throne ostensibly as protector of the king's children. He then killed the children and sired [sons who later succeeded him on the throne].[29]

Some of the Indian sources add that Mahapadma's lowliness of birth outraged rulers in neighboring kingdoms, who were all members of the Kshatriya caste. They derisively called him a "destroyer of the princely order."[30]

These words, meant in the figurative sense, turned out to be prophetic in the literal sense because Mahapadma ended up destroying most of the princes who had insulted him. After carefully and skillfully organizing a large military force, he invaded and seized control of several neighboring states. The exact size of the territories he overran is unknown. But some of his immediate successors built on his conquests. And at its greatest extent, the Nanda Empire covered a large portion of northern India stretching from the Bay of Bengal in the east to the outer edges of the Indus Valley in the west.

Mahapadma's successors were able to build on and maintain this empire because they had inherited his formida-

The King Goes Hunting

While serving as Seleucus's ambassador to Chandragupta's royal court in Magadha, the Greek writer Megasthenes closely observed Indian customs. In this surviving excerpt from his Indika, Megasthenes describes the elaborate ceremonies surrounding a royal hunt.

Crowds of women surround him [the king], and outside of this circle spearmen are ranged. The road is marked off with ropes, and it is death, for man and woman alike, to pass within the ropes. Men with drums and gongs lead the procession. The king hunts in the enclosures and shoots arrows from a platform. At his side stand two or three armed women. If he hunts in the open grounds he shoots from the back of an elephant. Of the women, some are in chariots, some on horses, and some even on elephants, and they are equipped with weapons of every kind, as if they were going on a campaign.

Megasthenes, *Indika,* surviving fragments collected in J.W. McCrindle, ed. and trans., *Ancient India Described by Megasthenes and Arrian.* Calcutta: Tracker, Spink, 1877, excerpted at: http://www.mssu.edu/projectsouthasia/history/primarydocs/Foreign_Views/GreekRoman/Megasthenes-Indika.htm

ble army. Under the command of the last Nanda king, Dhana Nanda, who ruled in the 320 B.C., it was the great military force that Alexander's men heard about and were reluctant to fight. According to one of Alexander's principal ancient biographers, the first-century A.D. Greek Plutarch, the region controlled by Magadha

swarmed with a gigantic host of infantry, horsemen, and elephants. It was said that the [ruler of the king-

dom] was waiting for Alexander's attack with an army of 80,000 cavalry, 200,000 infantry, 8,000 chariots, and 6,000 fighting elephants.[31]

These figures were undoubtedly exaggerated. Curtius's figures of 20,000 cavalry, 200,000 infantry, 2,000 chariots, and 3,000 elephants may also be too high. But even if the Magadhan army was only half as big as Curtius reported, it was still enormous by ancient standards; and this

A terra-cotta bust of the head of a smiling boy from the Mauryan period, the time in which Chandragupta ascended to power.

explains why the Greeks were not very eager to tangle with it.

Accession of Chandragupta

The Nandas were apparently not as successful in their domestic affairs as they were in their conquests. The Indian sources for this period mention repeated government corruption, court intrigues, royal murders, and rising discontent among the populace. Such a situation naturally created an opening for an ambitious and talented individual to step in and seize power. And this is exactly what transpired. Sometime in the early 320s B.C. a man named Chandragupta Maurya, perhaps a member of the Vaishya caste, joined forces with a Brahmin named Kautilya. The latter had earlier been a member of the Nanda court but had recently become Dhana Nanda's enemy. Chandragupta and Kautilya tried to oust the emperor but were unsuccessful and had to flee.

The two schemers remained undaunted, however. They and their hard-core followers gathered an army of disgruntled citizens from various outlying regions of the Nanda realm and in about 321 B.C. launched a far larger rebellion. After overrunning "the outlying provinces of the Nanda kingdom," John Keay writes, the rebels

eventually converged on Magadha. [The capital of] Pataliputra was probably besieged and, aided no doubt by defectors, the [rebels] triumphed. The last Nanda was sent packing, quite literally. He is supposed to have been spared only his life, plus [any] of his legendary wealth as he could crate and carry away, [and] Chandragupta Maurya ascended the Magadhan throne.[32]

Chandragupta Maurya was perhaps just twenty-five when he took power in Magadha, and he had no experience as a national leader. Yet from the start he proved himself a skilled and effective ruler. This was almost certainly partly attributable to the advice he continued to get from his friend and confidant Kautilya, who was a political theorist of the first order. Kautilya wrote a book on statecraft—the *Arthashastra* (meaning "science of material gain"), which has survived. It describes an effective ruler as one who takes an active role in all government affairs and puts the good of the country and citizenry above his own. "If a king is energetic, his subjects will be equally energetic," Kautilya declared. And by contrast:

If he is reckless, they will not only be reckless likewise, but also eat into his works. Besides, a reckless king will easily fall into the hands of his enemies. . . . In the happiness of his subjects lies his happiness; in their welfare his welfare; whatever pleases himself he shall not consider as good, but whatever pleases his subjects he shall consider as good. Hence the king shall ever be active and discharge his duties; the root of wealth is activity, and of evil its reverse.[33]

An early example of a Mauryan creation goddess, carved in the 2nd-century B.C. when Chandragupta was conquering most of northern India.

Chandragupta seems to have done his best to live by these words. The fourth-century Greek writer Megasthenes, who lived for some time in the Mauryan court, said that the Indian raja was a tireless and attentive sovereign:

> He remains in court for the whole day, without allowing the business to be interrupted, even though the hour arrives when he must needs attend to his person. . . . He continues [holding audiences with his subjects] while [a massage] performed by four attendants is still proceeding.[34]

The Indian Julius Caesar?

It was not by chance that Megasthenes found himself at the Mauryan court. He got there as the result of the following series of events.

Shortly after taking Magadha's throne, Chandragupta took advantage of the formidable army he had inherited from the Nandas and launched large-scale military expeditions. By about 311 B.C. he had gained control of all the lands stretching from Magadha westward to the Indus River, including some of the territories Alexander had seized only two decades before. Chandragupta's chief Greek opponent in the struggle for these territories was Alexander's former general Seleucus, who now controlled Mesopotamia, Iran, Bactria, and parts of the western Indus Valley.

After some bloody fighting, in which the Mauryians seem to have gotten the upper hand, the two sides agreed to make peace. Chandragupta (whom the Greeks called Sandrokottos) and Seleucus signed a treaty in 305 B.C. In it the Greek king ceded a large swath of former Greek lands west of the Indus to Chandragupta, in return for five hundred war elephants and a dynastic alliance. (Either a Greek princess married a Mauryan prince or a Mauryan princess married a Greek prince; the ancient sources are unclear on this point.) Seleucus also sent Megasthenes as his ambassador to the Mauryan court. Megasthenes later described that court and other aspects of India and its culture in a book titled *Indika*, small sections of which have survived as quotes in the books of later ancient writers.

Overall Chandragupta's conquests were spectacular. He eventually held sway over almost all of northern India. And later western writers came to call him the "Indian Julius Caesar," in reference to the famous Roman general who conquered Gaul (what is now France). Perhaps Chandragupta might have pressed on with his army. The rich kingdom of Kalinga, lying south of Magadha, was still independent, as were the Deccan kingdoms. But in 301 B.C. the king suddenly abdicated his throne, became a poor monk (in the Jain faith, founded in India more than two centuries before), and starved himself to death; his son Bindusara then became raja. Or at least this is the official story recorded in the ancient sources. Some modern scholars think that abruptly giving up power that way was out of character for Chandragupta. They suspect that Bindusara somehow eliminated his father and concocted a cover story.

In whatever manner Bindusara gained the throne, he reigned until 269 B.C., a total of about thirty-two years. Little of a concrete nature is known about his personal life. But there is no question that, like his father, he was an ambitious and skilled soldier. Bindusara expanded the empire by conquering large portions of the Deccan.

Aśoka's Military and Moral Conquests

At the close of Bindusara's reign, the Mauryan Empire was bigger than any native Indian nation or empire had ever been. Yet it was destined to grow still larger under his son and successor, Aśoka, whom posterity came to see as the greatest ruler of the dynasty. When Bindusara died his several sons fought over possession of the throne. Aśoka (whose name means "The Sorrowless One") emerged

The column of Aśoka in India. Aśoka was the greatest ruler of the Mauryan dynasty.

Duties of Government Superintendents

In his Arthashastra, Kautilya laid out an incredibly detailed guide to setting up what he saw as an efficient and fair government. It included a number of national departments similar in many respects to those in modern nations. Each department was headed by a superintendent. There were superintendents of agriculture, commerce, grain storehouses, weights and measures, toll collection, cows, horses, elephants, prostitutes, and more. Here are only a few of the duties of and rules enforced by the superintendent of ships.

The superintendent of ships shall examine the accounts relating to navigation not only on oceans and mouths of rivers, but also on lakes natural or artificial, and rivers. . . . Villages on seashores or on the banks of rivers and lakes shall pay a fixed amount of tax. Fishermen shall give 1/6th of their haul as fees for fishing license. Merchants shall pay the customary toll levied in port-towns. Passengers arriving on board the king's ship shall pay the requisite amount of sailing fees. . . . Pirate ships, vessels which are bound for the country of an enemy, as well as those which have violated the customs and rules in force in port towns shall be destroyed. . . . Brahmins, monks, children, the aged, the afflicted, royal messengers, and pregnant women shall be provided by the superintendent with free passes to cross rivers.

Kautilya, *Arthashastra,* Book 2, trans. R. Shamasastry. http://www.mssu.edu/projectsouthasia/ history/primarydocs/Arthashastra/BookII.htm

victorious sometime in the early-to-mid 260s B.C.

From the start the young emperor was determined to conquer Kalinga, the only important kingdom in India not yet under Mauryan control. In about 260 B.C. he launched a full-scale invasion of Kalinga, whose inhabitants were completely overwhelmed. Ancient sources describe an enormous bloodbath in which 100,000 were killed. Another 150,000 Kalingans were captured or driven from their homes, and thousands more died of illness or starvation in the months that followed.

Then something extraordinary happened. Having attained his most cherished goal and become the most powerful man in India's history, Aśoka had a change of heart. When he held the mangled bodies of the dead and witnessed the terrible suffering of the shattered families and communities, he was horrified and sincerely remorseful. Moreover he had the courage and depth of character to admit it to all his subjects. Aśoka had messages

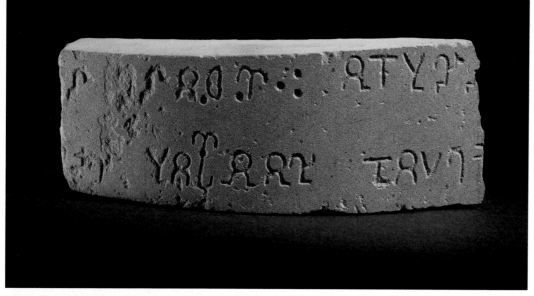

An edict, or order, of Aśoka, written in Brahmi script. Aśoka had messages inscribed on rocks and pillars across his empire.

inscribed on rocks and pillars across his empire, saying in part:

> [I am] deeply pained by the killing, dying and deportation that take place when an unconquered country is conquered. But [I am] pained even more [when that country's people] are injured, killed or separated from their loved ones. Even those who are not affected by all this suffer when they see friends, acquaintances, companions and relatives affected. These misfortunes befall all as a result of war, and this pains [me]. Therefore the killing, death or deportation of a hundredth, or even a thousandth part of those who died during the conquest of Kalinga now pains [me]. Truly, [I believe that] non-injury, restraint, and impartiality to all beings [is a more moral policy].[35]

In keeping with this new, more humane philosophy, Aśoka converted to Buddhism, which preaches nonviolent treatment of all living things. Across his vast empire he instituted the Buddhist concept of dharma (or dhamma), roughly translated as "moral conquest" or "moral law." In another inscription Aśoka described it as always striving for "goodness, kindness, generosity, truthfulness, and purity." At the same time people should try to avoid "violence, cruelty, anger, pride, and jealousy." In so doing, he said, they will find "happiness in this world and the next."[36] Ruling within the constraints of dharma,

Aśoka forbade the slaughter of animals, which significantly reduced meat-eating in India. He also promoted Buddhism by sending missionaries far and wide to spread the faith's nonviolent, humane tenets. Yet simultaneously he urged religious toleration, saying that all faiths are worthy of respect. "It is better to honor other religions," he said in one of his rock inscriptions.

> By so doing, one's own religion benefits, and so do other religions, while doing otherwise harms one's own religion and the religions of others. Whoever praises his own religion, due to excessive devotion, and condemns others with the thought "Let me glorify my own religion," only harms his own religion. Therefore contact between religions is good. One should listen to and respect the doctrines professed by others.[37]

In addition Aśoka tried to improve his people's welfare by creating hospitals, roads, fountains, and gardens. Finally he adhered to the *Arthashastra*'s principles of fair and efficient government introduced during his grandfather's reign.

Mauryan Accomplishments and Legacy

Unfortunately for Aśoka's subjects, his successors were far less capable and successful than he was. For the most part, the seven men who sat on the Mauryan throne following his death in 232 B.C. lacked his vision, skills, sense of humanity, and sheer boldness of leadership. As

Part of the Maruryan legacy consisted of art and architecture like this three-headed lion pillar.

a result they were unable to maintain either the happiness and respect of their people or the integrity of the realm. The empire steadily shrank as rebellions erupted and its outlying provinces broke away and declared their independence. Finally the dynasty came to an inglorious end in 184 B.C. when the commander of the army assassinated the last Mauryan ruler, Brihadratha.

Though the Mauryans were gone, they left behind a formidable legacy, parts of which helped to shape the character of India in later ages. They had created the

Customs of the Dharma

In this passage from one of Aśoka's rock inscriptions, he lists some of the ceremonies, or customs, of the dharma and explains why they are superior to other customs.

The ceremony of the Dharma . . . involves proper behavior towards servants and employees, respect for teachers, restraint towards living beings, and generosity towards monks and Brahmins. These and other things constitute the ceremony of the Dharma. Therefore a father, a son, a brother, a master, a friend, a companion, and even a neighbor should say: "This is good, this is the ceremony that should be performed until its purpose is fulfilled, [so] this I shall do." Other ceremonies are of doubtful fruit, for they may achieve their purpose, or they may not, and even if they do, it is only in this world. But the ceremony of the Dharma is timeless. Even if it does not achieve its purpose in this world, it produces great merit in the next, whereas if it does achieve its purpose in this world, one gets great merit both here and there.

Aśoka's 13th Rock Inscription, in "The Edicts of King Aśoka," trans. Ven S. Dhammika. http://www.cs.colostate.edu/~malaiya/ashoka.html

first political unit that embraced nearly the entire Indian subcontinent. Though no one was able to repeat this accomplishment until modern times, as Keay says, "the ideal of a pan-Indian empire was never forgotten,"[38] and remained an inspiration to later Indians.

A more tangible part of the Mauryan legacy consisted of architecture, art, and large-scale physical infrastructure that lasted for generations to come and influenced later Indian cultures. Aśoka's huge palace, for instance, was still standing six centuries later when a Chinese visitor named Fa-hsien saw it and wrote about it. The structure was beautifully decorated with gold and silver trim and elaborate sculptures, he said. It stood in the Mauryan capital of Pataliputra, which Megasthenes called the largest city in the world. The city stretched for miles along the banks of the Ganges and featured a mighty defensive wall with 570 towers and 64 gates; well-planned streets; wide marketplaces; and a number of public meeting places and facilities for horse-racing. The techniques of stone masonry used in Pataliputra were adopted by later Indian builders. In addition a Mauryan royal road that ran some 1,150 miles (1,850km) from the city westward across northern India remained in use into modern times. Furthermore the modern nation of India adopted as its emblem the elegant cluster of four lions that Aśoka's artisans carved atop the pillars bearing his inscriptions.

Perhaps the biggest and most profound aspect of the Mauryan legacy, though, was Aśoka's championing of Buddhism. His missionaries traveled not only to every section of the subcontinent, but also into neighboring lands. As a result the faith eventually spread across all of eastern Asia and became one of the world's great religions.

Meanwhile Hinduism and Jainism remained strong in India and continued to gain followers. Indeed it is remarkable that not long before the Mauryans' rise to power, India had produced three major religions destined to survive to the present. Moreover this achievement, one of the most important contributions made to world culture by any nation, had occurred in the amazingly short span of a few centuries.

Chapter Five

India's Three Great Religions

One way that India was unique among ancient civilizations was that it gave rise to no less than three faiths that stood the test of time and became great world religions. From the subcontinent's fertile cultural and spiritual soil sprang Hinduism and not long afterward Buddhism and Jainism. The Hindu faith developed directly from Vedic beliefs and rituals, the roots of which stretched back into the third millennium B.C. or perhaps even earlier. The Vedic religion changed steadily over time as new ideas and gods were added. This evolution produced the more mature and complex version known as Hinduism during the period in which the Mahajanapadas arose (the early first millennium B.C.).

Hinduism was therefore based on and continued to embrace traditional religious concepts and gods from the past. Yet in a more general sense, Indian spiritual thought remained flexible and tolerant and allowed still newer ideas to thrive.

Some of these new concepts and beliefs inspired the emergence of Buddhism and Jainism beginning in circa 500–450 B.C. These faiths did not reject Vedic-Hindu religious traditions outright. Rather they retained many of them while altering others. Those altered beliefs and rituals were mainly concerned with providing people with new ways of finding heavenly truth and liberating the soul. Thereafter the three faiths coexisted in the subcontinent for the rest of ancient times. (Buddhism largely disappeared from India later, partly as a result of large-scale Muslim invasions.)

Vedic Beliefs and Rituals

Exactly when and how the Vedic faith—the ancient precursor of Hinduism, Buddhism, and Jainism—got started will probably never be known. The precise beliefs and rituals of the early Vedic faith are also uncertain, although some of those of late Vedic times still exist in

Hindu worship. What seems clear is that over the course of many centuries the Vedic religion underwent slow but steady change.

This evolution in religious concepts and rituals can be seen in the adoption of new gods over time. In each instance the older gods were never discarded; instead priests and worshipers kept them, usually assigning them less prominent roles in the cosmic and spiritual order, or *Rta*. The earliest chief Vedic, or perhaps even pre-Vedic, deity was Dyaus. Roughly equivalent to the Greek Zeus, he was a sky god who could control the weather and command the forces of thunder and lightning. A few of the hymns in the Rig-Veda mention him, but by the time these hymns were composed he was no longer the main god.

Dyaus was demoted to the role of a more distant divine father-figure as his son, Varuna, became the chief deity. Also a sky god, Varuna oversaw the underworld, too. The Rig-Veda pictures Varuna as both supremely holy and wise, as well as powerful. One hymn says in part:

[The far-seeing Varuna] knows the path of birds that fly through heaven, and [he] knows the pathway of the . . . high and mighty wind [and] he knows the Gods who dwell above. Varuna, true to holy law, sits down among his people; he, most wise, sits there to govern all [and] he beholds all wondrous things, both what have been and what hereafter will be done.[39]

Varouna, Dieu des Eaux.

Varuna was both a sky god, and oversaw the underworld. The Rig-Veda pictures Varuna as supremely holy, wise, and powerful.

In Hinduism, Lord Ganesha is the elephant-headed god of wisdom and learning.

Eventually, the Vedic faith adopted another of Dyaus's sons, Indra, as its chief god. In the Vedic myths Indra defeated a powerful demon named Vritra, thereby allowing sunlight and water to invigorate the earth and make human life possible. Worship of Indra and the other Vedic gods did not take place in temples, which appeared later in India. Instead hearth-like altars were erected to accommodate the main ritual of worship—fire sacrifices. Guided, it was thought, by the fire god, Agni, Brahmin priests led people in lighting sacred fires and chanting hymns, acts that supposedly appeased the gods and purified the worshipers.

Hinduism and the Universal Spirit

As classical Hinduism emerged, it retained hymn-chanting, fire rituals, and other aspects of Vedic worship. However, the Hindus added some important new concepts. First they introduced a creator-god—Brahma, who was also the basis for a different way of thinking about the gods in general. The older Vedic gods had been part of a traditional polytheistic belief system, in which people worshiped several separate divine entities.

In contrast a majority of ancient Hindus came to view Brahma as a sort of overriding universal spirit, the *ishvara* (or *ishwara*). This spirit had the ability to manifest itself in different ways, taking on various alternate faces and guises. Among these guises might be other Hindu gods, including Shiva, god of destruction; Vishnu, the preserver and governor of the universe; and Ganesh

(or Ganesha), the elephant-headed god of wisdom and learning. Similarly each of these deities could manifest himself in different forms. Vishnu, for example, took several earthly guises, or incarnations, among them Rama (who appears in the *Ramayana*) and Krishna (a major character in the *Bhagavad-Gita*, a part of the *Mahabharata*). In addition to these various divine manifestations, the Hindus recognized a number of separate heavenly beings. These included the *devas*, somewhat equivalent to angels, and the *asuras*, or demons. Thus ancient Hinduism intricately combined various aspects of monotheism and polytheism.

Ancient Hinduism also placed a strong emphasis on the concept of reincarnation (*samsara*), or repeated rebirth of the human soul (the *atman*). The belief was that the soul is immortal. When someone's body died, the soul passed into another body, and this process repeated itself as the soul strived to better itself and become one with the universal spirit. Meanwhile the circumstances and experiences of each successive lifetime, or incarnation, depended on karma, a merciless law of moral consequences. Sinharaja Tammita-Delgoda explains:

> Karma governed the relationship between one's actions in one incarnation and one's station in the next. Merit was rewarded, but sin had to be atoned for. Thus, the merit and the sins of the past life were visited on the next. According to karma, we are what we are because of what we were and what we did.[40]

The Indestructible Soul

The Bhagavad-Gita is one of Hinduism's sacred texts. Consisting of about seven hundred verses, it is only a small part of the much larger Mahabharata, an epic poem describing a great civil conflict in the Vedic Age. Essentially the Bhagavad-Gita is a lecture by Krishna, an incarnation of the god Vishnu, who has come to earth to take part in the war. In this excerpt he urges the humans to fight, telling them that they need not fear death because their souls will live on.

Neither for the dead nor those not dead do the wise grieve. Never was there a time when I did not exist, nor you nor these lords of men. Neither will there be a time when we shall not exist; we all exist from now on. As the soul experiences in this body childhood, youth, and old age, so also it acquires another body. [Sensations like] cold, heat, pleasure, pain . . . are impermanent; you must endure them. . . . Know that indestructible essence by which all this is pervaded. No one is able to cause the destruction of the imperishable [soul]. These bodies have an end; it is the indestructible, infinite soul that it is eternal.

Bhagavad-Gita, 2, trans. Sanderson Beck. http://www.san.beck.org/Gita.html

These concepts reinforced the caste system, which divided people into groups of varying status, moral worth, and level of material comforts. Someone who did disreputable things in one lifetime could be expected to be born into a lower caste in the next life and vice versa.

To establish oneself as a reputable person worshipers had to demonstrate their devotion to God through regular performance of standard rituals of worship (*puja*). This could be done in a temple, with the aid of priests. In fact erecting large, elaborately decorated temples was seen as a way of showing people's dedication to divine forces and righteous living. Worshipers could also perform the rituals at home using small makeshift shrines. These most often featured icons (*murti*), statues or paintings symbolizing chosen gods. The rituals included chanting, placing food offerings on the shrine, reading from the Vedas, *Ramayana*, or other Hindu

An 80-foot-tall Buddha statue looms over the horizon in Bodhgaya, India. The teachings of Buddhism are based on the life and teachings of a man who became known as Buddha, "the enlightened one."

scriptures, lighting candles and burning incense, and/or meditation.

Buddhism's Search for Wisdom

Like the Hindus, the ancient Buddhists had temples, priests, and scriptures and believed in the existence of various heavenly beings. However, Buddhists viewed these beings not as controllers of the cosmic order but as part of it, along with humans, and therefore equally subject to its laws. Furthermore, the Buddhists did not recognize an all-powerful creator god. A philosophy, or way of seeing life, as well as a religion, Buddhism became a path to the discovery of true knowledge and peace with oneself, one's community, and the larger universe. A Buddhist could find that path with the aid of priests. Or he or she could do it alone, as an individual seeking salvation through the attainment of wisdom. In that way each person had the potential to become an instrument of his or her own fate.

Buddhism was based on the life and teachings of a man who became known as Buddha, or "the Buddha," meaning "the enlightened one." The actual details of his life are shrouded by a veil of mystery and legend. Parts of the story that developed about him in Indian tradition may be true or almost so, while other parts are likely exaggerated or fabricated. That story begins with his birth as Siddhartha Gautama, a prince in one of India's northern kingdoms. The traditional date for this event is 563 B.C., but many modern scholars suspect he was born somewhat later, perhaps about 500 B.C.

As a child and young man Siddhartha led the happy, comfortable life of a royal person and knew nothing of the existence of disease, suffering, and death. But at age twenty-nine he left the palace and began exploring the countryside. There, to his shock and dismay, he witnessed old age and its infirmities, sickness, and death and learned that these are normal, inevitable aspects of life.

This experience changed Siddhartha's own life forever. He decided to devote himself to solitude and meditation, as Hindu monks did. Adopting an existence of extreme self-discipline and self-denial, he neglected and punished his body, hoping this would help his mind to focus better on finding life's truths. But then he realized that abusing his body was pointless and unproductive and only clouded his thinking. He later told his followers that suffering "produces confusion and sickly thoughts." It would be better to "keep the body in good health," and thereby "keep our mind strong and clear."[41]

The Eightfold Path

In fact Siddhartha sensed that finding the causes of suffering and how to alleviate it were the keys to attaining true wisdom. He searched for a long time, and then one day he had an epiphany, or sudden realization. Thus having achieved enlightenment he became the Buddha. He saw that there are four basic, overriding truths surrounding human existence, the first being that life is filled with suffering. Second, suffering is the result of arrogance, self-indulgence, and greed,

Sculpted Images of the Buddha

Those ancient peoples who adopted the Buddha's philosophy were often inspired to celebrate the faith and its ideas in art, including sculpture. At first it was considered disrespectful to carve statues, or icons, showing Buddha's specific physical form. In this "aniconic" phase of Buddhist sculpture, artisans instead carved objects indirectly associated with the great prophet. These included a "wheel of law," depicting the great truths Buddha had discovered; sculptures of the sacred tree beneath which the prophet found enlightenment; and casts of feet and footprints symbolizing the spread of Buddhist ideas far and wide.

By the first century A.D., however, it was no longer forbidden to show images of Buddha. And in the centuries that followed, peoples across the Far East carved or cast statues of Buddha, some of them gigantic. In China, Japan, and other areas of the Far East, Buddhist themes combined with and complemented traditional ones in sculpture and other forms of artistic expression.

and third, these ills are not inevitable and can be overcome.

The fourth and most profound truth revealed by the Buddha consisted of the means of overcoming the causes of suffering. It was a code of conduct that he called the Eightfold Path. The eight steps in the path are right views (or understanding), right aspiration (or purpose), right speech, right behavior, right vocation (or livelihood), right effort, right thoughts (or awareness), and right contemplation (or concentration, or meditation). Also, he said, people should not kill any living thing. Nor should they steal, lie, get drunk, or have sex outside of marriage. By strictly following these steps and good behaviors, the Buddha advocated, one

could attain Nirvana, a state of selflessness, peace, and happiness. One would also escape from the relentless cycle of reincarnation.

The Buddha went out and preached these ideas, which became increasingly popular. Many Hindus had no problem reconciling the concepts of right living and meditation with existing Hindu doctrines. So numerous Indians accepted basic Buddhist doctrines without giving up all their former beliefs, constituting still another example of continuity in Indian thought and society.

Well after the Buddha's death, during the reign of the Mauryan ruler A oka, Buddhist missionaries carried these ideas beyond India's borders. Eventually

Thousands of devotees make their way to the feet of the 58.8-foot monolithic Jain statue of Gomateshwara (Lord Bahubali) at Shravanabelagola, India, in 2006. The statue glows red from applications of vermilion from the faithful.

Buddhism spread to China, Cambodia, Thailand, Korea, and Japan. As had been the case with many Indian Hindus, these foreign peoples often found ways to accept Buddhist philosophy while retaining some of their former religious beliefs.

Jainism and the Soul's Liberation

Escaping the remorseless cycle of reincarnation and achieving liberation and ultimate knowledge were also basic tenets of Jainism. The founding father, so to speak, of Jainism was roughly a contemporary of the Buddha, although it is unclear which man began preaching first. Also like the Buddha, the founder of Jainism, Vardhamana, known as Mahavira (or "Great Hero"), started out as a prince leading a privileged life. Mahavira, too, gave up his worldly life at about the age of thirty; began living a monk-like existence of self-discipline and self-denial; and eventually underwent an intellectual and spiritual transformation.

Mahavira's enlightenment consisted in part of the knowledge that all life is potentially divine, in the sense that all living things, not just humans, have souls. Therefore it is wrong to kill people, animals, and even insects. Also, people could escape the cycle of reincarnation by achieving the liberation (*moksha*) of their souls. To achieve this one's soul had to be disentangled from karma. Unlike the Hindus and Buddhists, the Jains viewed karma as the material of which the universe is

Followers of Jainism believe it is wrong to kill people, animals, and even insects. Here, a Jain nun wears a mask to cover her mouth, hoping to prevent the accidental killing of any insects that may fly into her mouth.

made, and the goal was to escape from karma's grip and reach a heavenly level above and beyond it. There they would become *siddhas,* beings devoid of suffering and ignorance.

This process of liberation, the Jains came to believe, could be accomplished only by following certain disciplines and righteous acts. To teach ordinary people the proper behaviors, at various moments in history *Jinas,* also called *tirthankaras,* appeared. These were special humans who had achieved enlightenment and gained ultimate knowledge. *Jains* believed that Mahavira was one of the Jinas. He taught two sets of vows, or rules of right behavior. The first, the Great Vows *(Mahavratas),* were for Jain monks, who led more disciplined lives than laypeople (ordinary folk). As John Bowker,

a noted scholar of comparative religions, explains, these vows included:

> nonviolence, speaking the truth, abstaining from sexual activity, not taking anything that is not given, and detachment [living apart] from persons, places, and things. . . . Laypeople take a parallel set of vows, known as *anuvratas,* or lesser vows, which apply the five vows to life in the world. These are that laypeople should be vegetarian and should not do work that involves the deliberate destruction of life, such as hunting or fishing.[42]

Six occupations emerged that were considered acceptable for Jains to adopt: farming, government work, writing,

Mahavira Becomes a Monk

In these excerpts from one of the main Jain scriptures, the Kalpa Sutra, the former prince Mahavira, now turned monk, gives up his earthly possessions and becomes the object of thousands of adoring followers.

He possessed supreme, unlimited, unimpeded knowledge and intuition. The venerable monk Mahavira perceived with this his supreme unlimited knowledge and intuition that the time for his renunciation [of worldly possessions] had come. He left his silver, he left his gold, he left his riches, corn, majesty, and kingdom; his army, grain, treasure, storehouse, town [and] subjects. . . . Then the venerable monk Mahavira gazed on by a circle of thousands of eyes, praised by a circle of thousands of mouths, extolled by a circle of thousands of hearts, being the object of many thousands of wishes, desired because of his splendor, beauty, and virtues.

Kalpa Sutra, 4th Lecture, trans. Hermann Jacobi. http://www.ishwar.com/jainism/holy_kalpa_sutra/texts02.html

artistic endeavors, craft work, and commerce.

Like Buddhism, Jainism appealed to many Indians and the new belief system spread steadily through the subcontinent. At first Jain ideals were taught by Mahavira's twelve disciples, who collected his teachings into the earliest Jain scriptures. Among them are the Kalpa Sutra (Book of Ritual) and the Tatthavartha Sutra (Book of Reality). In the Jain philosophy contained in these writings, liberated souls attained a pure state of infinite knowledge, perception, and happiness—in a sense a divine-like state. So there was no need to invoke a separate god to bestow these blessings; and like Buddhism, Jainism had no universal creator god. Most Jains did acknowledge the existence of the Hindu deities. But they saw these gods as subject to the same natural laws and processes as humans, including reincarnation and the quest for liberation.

By the time of the rise of the Mauryan Empire in the late fourth century B.C., therefore, India had a complex and humane religious culture. Basic Hindu beliefs had been greatly enriched by Buddhist and Jain philosophical ideas, and feelings of religious tolerance pervaded society. This openness to new ideas encouraged the formation of differing schools of thought within all three faiths during the centuries that followed, including the so-called golden age that began in the fourth century A.D.

Chapter Six

The Guptas and the Golden Age

After Aśoka's death in 232 B.C., the Mauryan Empire rapidly fell apart and officially ceased to exist in 184 B.C. Now highly fragmented, as it had been before the rise of the Mauryans, India witnessed a long period of political disunity as numerous local dynasties and rulers rose and fell. Modern scholars often refer to these states and royal families as the early "Middle Kingdoms." Among others they included Magadha, now ruled by the Mauryans' successors; Kalinga, which had regained its independence; the Indo-Greek kingdom established by the Bactrian Greeks Demetrius and Menander; some moderately powerful kingdoms in the Deccan; and a series of dynasties of central Asian origin that ruled in the subcontinent's northwestern sector.

Finally in the early 300s, the greatest of the Middle Kingdoms, the Gupta Empire, arose. Its rulers managed to unite northern India into an imperial realm that rivaled, though was never quite as large as, that of the Mauryans. The Guptas reigned over an age of widespread peace and prosperity, and its rulers championed the arts and sciences. The era's artistic and literary flowering, along with advances in mathematics, astronomy, philosophy, medicine, and other intellectual endeavors, inspired modern historians to call it India's cultural "golden age."

The Early Middle Kingdoms

Though the Gupta period boasted major political unity, prosperity, and cultural achievements, the earlier Middle Kingdoms had not languished in some kind of dark age. To the contrary, though politically disunited and often war-torn, most of these pre-Gupta states were quite prosperous and culturally rich. The Shunga (or Sunga) dynasty in Magadha is a clear illustration. Its founder, Pusyamitra Shunga, was the Magadhan military

A stupa, or temple, from the Sunga dynasty, a prosperous and culturally rich period in India's history.

general who assassinated the last Mauryan ruler. He and his successors, who ruled for a little more than a century, frequently warred with the Kalingans, the Indo-Greeks, and others. Yet trade went on all across India, producing much of the wealth that financed these conflicts. The Shungas sponsored many cultural endeavors as well, including education, literature, fine arts, and the building of many splendid Buddhist temples. Moreover many of these programs continued under the next Magadhan dynasty—the Kanva. The Kanvas overthrew the Shungas in 72 B.C. and ruled the country for roughly a century.

A similar situation developed in the mid-Deccan region. There Simuka, the first ruler of the Andhra (or Satavahana) dynasty, broke free of Mauryan control shortly after A oka's death. The Andhras lorded over a prosperous and successful kingdom for more than four centuries. Like the Magadhans, Kalingans, and other northern neighbors, they engaged in many wars. Yet the Andhra kings were big supporters of the arts, including their sponsorship of poetry and other literature and the erection of several Buddhist temples bearing magnificent sculptures. They were also the first native Indian rulers to issue coins bearing images of kings' faces (an idea copied from the Greeks).

Meanwhile northwestern India, including the Indus Valley, endured an influx of foreign rulers beginning in the early first century B.C. First came the Shakas (or Sakas), which modern scholars sometimes call the Indo-Scythians. Apparently a Caucasian people, they came from central Asia and destroyed the Greek Bactrian kingdom on their way into India. Not long afterward another wave of Caucasian Asians followed—the Yuezhi, who came to be called the Kushans. They displaced the Shaka kings, some of whom moved into the southern Indus Valley and ruled there for several centuries. Modern scholars call these Shaka descendants the "Western Satraps."

However, the idea of a large-scale Kushan invasion of India—implying major population movements and disruptions—must be viewed with caution. As John Keay points out, "India's ancient history was first reconstructed largely by British scholars in the nineteenth century, who, schooled on the invasions of Aryans, Macedonians, and Muslims [in India's medieval period], readily detected a pattern of incursions." Thus, although some kind of Kushan invasion may well have occurred, it is also possible that the Kushans "may have come initially as allies or mercenaries, invited by disaffected Indians . . . or they may have come as refugees fleeing invasions [of their own homelands]."[43]

More certain is that after the Kushans arrived in western India, they acquired political control. The Kushan rulers also converted to Buddhism and became eager patrons of the arts and literature. In sculpture, for instance, they promoted and provided the money for the creation of numerous paintings and large statues of the Buddha. Yet they did not impose Asian artistic styles on the painters and sculptors; rather the Kushans allowed the then ongoing merger of native Indian and Greek artistic styles to prevail. The result was a unique and fruitful joint artistic effort among members of three quite different cultures. The Kushans, Keay writes, who controlled

east-west trade in Bactria, as well as vast territories in India, had wealth to lavish on both the new faith [Buddhism, which was new to the Kushans] and the new art [the style of which] developed rapidly, influencing architecture and painting, and inspiring a narrative art based on Buddhist legend but using Greek compositions and mannerisms. [This produced] a curious synthesis [combining] of Kushan patronage, Greek forms, and Indian inspiration. In sculpture, stucco [decorative plaster work], engraving, and painting, it was this synthesis which [provided] the inspiration for later Buddhist art in China and beyond.[44]

Rise of the Guptas

The arts and literature, as well as commerce and prosperity, reached an even higher point under the Gupta rulers. Their exact origins and the manner in which they established their dynasty in Magadha remain uncertain and are debated by scholars. The most prevalent theory is that they were from Bengal, the region lying directly east of Magadha. In

Walking in the Buddha's Footsteps

One of the major reasons that the Chinese traveler Fa-hsien toured India was that he was a devout Buddhist and wanted to visit some of the original Buddhist sites, especially places where the Buddha was said to have lived. In this excerpt from Fa-hsien's travel guide, he describes his emotional visit to a hill on which the founder of his faith had preached.

The hall where Buddha preached his Law [spiritual tenets] has been destroyed, and only the foundations of the brick walls remain. On this hill the peak is beautifully green, and rises grandly up; it is the highest of all the five hills [in the area]. I bought incense, flowers, oil, and lamps, and hired two [local men] to carry them to the peak. When I got to it, I made offerings with the flowers and incense, and lighted the lamps when the darkness began to come on. I felt melancholy, but restrained my tears and said, "Here Buddha delivered [the Law]. I, Fa-hsien, was born when I could not meet with Buddha; and now I only see the footprints which he has left, and the place where he lived, and nothing more."

Fa-hsien, *Record of the Buddhist Kingdoms,* chap. 29, trans. James Legge. http://www.gutenberg.org/dirs/2/1/2/2124/2124.txt

about 320 B.C. the founder of the dynasty, Chandragupta I (not to be confused with the Mauryan ruler of the same name) gained power in Magadha perhaps partly by royal marriage and partly by military force.

In whatever manner he took the throne, Chandragupta immediately revealed an enormous ego and equally huge ambitions. He called himself "King of Kings" and set a goal of restoring the lost glories of the Mauryan Empire. The extent of his conquests, if any, are unknown. But they were probably limited because the first major Gupta military expansion occurred under his son, Samudragupta. Supposedly, as he lay dying in 335, Chandragupta told the young man, "You are worthy. Rule this world."[45]

Taking these words to heart, Samudragupta led large-scale military campaigns across northern India. Initially he enjoyed considerable success, adding territories stretching from the Punjab to the Bay of Bengal to his new empire. He did not fare as well against the Deccan kingdoms and Western Satraps, however, as both managed to resist Gupta domination. Samudragupta also distinguished himself in cultural endeavors. A musician and poet himself, he earned the nickname "the poet king" and spent large sums sponsoring other artists. Once again Pataliputra became India's principal cultural center, marking the beginning of the cultural golden age.

The Gupta Zenith

When Samudragupta died in 375 after a long and fruitful reign, one of his sons, Ramagupta, inherited the throne. But the young man did not remain in power long. His brother Chandragupta soon ousted him and took the title Chandragupta II (reigned 375–415). The manner in which the coup occurred is uncertain, but the legendary tale later celebrated in plays and other literature likely contains some kernels of truth. First, the story goes, Ramagupta attacked the Western Satraps, who defeated him and forced him to sign a humiliating treaty. As Sinharaja Tammita-Delgoda tells it:

> Ramagupta was compelled to surrender his wife, Dhruvadevi, as part of the peace terms. Outraged by this, his younger brother Chandragupta disguised himself as the queen and entered the [enemy] king's palace in her stead. He killed the king and became an instant hero. In doing so, however, he had made a bitter enemy of his brother and he found himself left with no alternative but to kill him, too. Having assassinated Ramagupta, he married Dhruvadevi and assumed the throne.[46]

Having taken control of the empire, Chandragupta brought it to its height of power and influence. He adopted the title Vikramaditya, meaning "he whose splendor equals the sun," and launched the first of several military campaigns against the Western Satraps. The size and composition of the army he employed in these expeditions is not precisely known. But scholars think its mainstays were a large corps of foot archers and several units of war elephants. Most archers used a sturdy bamboo bow that fired bamboo arrows with metal tips to great distances. Like medieval English longbows, these weapons could do severe damage to columns of charging horsemen. Noblemen and other wealthy Indian archers sometimes used steel bows. Archers also carried swords, which they used only if the enemy made it through the rain of arrows and attacked them man-to-man. Some archers fired from platforms mounted

A front view of a Gupta temple from the late 6th century.

atop elephants; and these great beasts were also trained to charge and trample enemy infantry.

Using such forces, by about 409 Chandragupta had achieved complete victory over the Western Satraps and brought all of western India to the Gupta fold. Although the Deccan kingdoms remained independent, Chandragupta gave one of his daughters in marriage to the strongest Deccan king; this ensured friendly relations and the extension of Gupta influence throughout the subcontinent.

This tremendous unity, coupled with several years of peace, allowed the Gupta government to concentrate on expanding the economy and promoting the welfare of the citizenry. Foreign visitors during this period were amazed at the level of prosperity, which modern historians think rivaled that of the Roman Empire at its height. The Chinese Buddhist Fahsien, who toured India between 405 and 411, was particularly impressed by the imperial heartland of Magadha. "The cities and towns of this country," he wrote, "are the greatest of all [those] in [India]. The inhabitants are rich and prosperous, and vie with one another in the practice of benevolence and righteousness."[47]

It is not likely that all Indians were "rich and prosperous," of course. But the Gupta administration apparently established some sort of welfare system to provide the poor, disabled, and others in need with a safety net. Fa-hsien observed:

In the cities [there are] houses for dispensing charity and medicines. All the poor and destitute in the country, orphans, widowers, and childless men, maimed people, and cripples, and all who are diseased, go to those houses, and are provided with every kind of help, and doctors examine their diseases. They get the food and medicines which their cases require, and are made to feel at ease.[48]

Gupta Culture

The frequent mention of medicines in this account is significant. It reflects the important strides made in the healing arts during the Gupta Age, part of a larger flurry of achievements in the arts and sciences.

Doctors became highly efficient at delivering babies by caesarean section, setting broken bones, grafting damaged skin, and other procedures. This medical knowledge eventually passed to Arab communities situated west of India, and from there to Europe.

Other scientific disciplines that thrived under the Guptas were mathematics and astronomy. Indian scholars devised the decimal system and the concept of zero in this period, knowledge that also later passed to the West via the Arabs. Meanwhile Gupta astronomers calculated the length of the solar year with a degree of accuracy greater than that achieved by ancient Greek astronomers. Furthermore like the Greeks, the Guptas recognized

Cave painting of Buddha in meditation made during the Gupta dynasty, from the Ajanta Caves in Maharashtra, India.

The King Depicted in Drama

Among the surviving works of the Gupta poet Kalidasa is a play titled Shakuntala, named for its lead character, an orphaned forest goddess who wins the heart of a king. In this excerpt the king, who is hunting in the forest, demonstrates his respect for some holy men he encounters.

King (hastily). Stop the chariot.

Charioteer. Yes, your Majesty. *(He does so. Enter a hermit with his pupil.)*

Hermit (lifting his hand). O King, this deer belongs to the hermitage. Why should his tender form expire, as blossoms perish in the fire? How could that gentle life endure the deadly arrow, sharp and sure? Restore your arrow to the quiver; to you were weapons lent the broken-hearted to deliver, not strike the innocent.

King (bowing low). It is done. *(He does so.)*

Hermit (joyfully). A deed worthy of you . . . [a] shining example of kings. May you beget a son to rule earth and heaven.

King *(bowing low).* I am thankful for a Brahmin's blessing.

Kalidasa, Shakuntala, Hunting Scene, trans. Arthur W. Ryder. http://www.sacred-texts.com/hin/sha/sha05.htm

that Earth is a sphere, partly by observing the planet's curved shadow on the moon's face during lunar eclipses.

In literature a number of talented writers were active in the Gupta Age. But by far the greatest was Kalidasa, a poet and playwright whom later western experts came to call the "Indian Shakespeare." Like Shakespeare, Kalidasa shrewdly and effectively explored the full range of human emotions and the nature of the human condition with a universality that transcends time and place. The following passage from Kalidasa's long poem, *The*

Birth of the War God, is a good example. Specifically, it describes a god's intense feelings of love for another divine being; yet on a larger level it captures feelings of romantic passion that people in all ages and times can relate to.

My breast is stained; I lay among the ashes
    Of him I loved with
    all a woman's powers;
Now let me lie where death-fire flames and flashes,
    As glad as on a bed of budding

flowers.
Sweet Spring, you came often
where we lay sleeping
   On blossoms, I and
   he whose life is sped;
Unto the end your friendly office
keeping,
   Prepare for me the last, the fiery
   bed.
And fan the flame to which I am
committed
   With southern winds;
   I would no longer stay;
You know well how slow the
moments flitted
   For Love, my love, when I was
   far away.[49]

Kalidasa's works, along with those of other writers of his era, are telling. They display the high level of literary development that usually occurs only in an advanced, stable culture that treasures

and promotes the arts and other civilized endeavors.

Decline of the Guptas

The stability of the Gupta realm was not as long-lasting as Chandragupta had hoped it would be, however. After his death in 415, the empire began a slow but steady decline. During the reign of his son, Kumaragupta, a fierce Asian people—the Huns—invaded western India and did widespread damage. (Some of the Huns proceeded westward, attacked Europe, and threatened Rome.)

Kumaragupta's son, Skandagupta (reigned 454–467) was able to decisively defeat the intruders. But a new wave of Huns, the White Huns, arrived in the closing years of the fifth century. Because of the ongoing decline of the Gupta realm, including its military, they managed to

The Nalanda University

Under the enlightened intellectual climate of Gupta-ruled India, education thrived, including schools of higher learning, which were located in large monasteries. The most famous university of the era was the one in the Buddhist monastery at Nalanda, in Bihar (in northeastern India). Established by King Kumaragupta in about A.D. 450, the huge complex of temples, classrooms, and dormitories supported some ten thousand students and two thousand teachers. A library containing numerous ancient Asian texts was situated inside a nine-story building. This remarkable institution attracted pupils not only from all parts of India, but also from Tibet, Korea, China, Japan, Persia, and elsewhere. The religious ideas and traditions promoted at Nalanda strongly influenced the later development of Buddhism in Tibet, Vietnam, China, and Japan.

ATTILA FLAGEL·DEI

Attila (406–453), leader of the Huns. The Huns' invasion of India led to the fall of the Gupta Empire.

seize the Punjab and then pushed eastward into the Ganges Valley.

(In a stark historical parallel, these events closely coincided with the fall of the Western Roman Empire in the 470s, also caused principally by "barbarian," or foreign, invasions).

A makeshift alliance of Indian kings was finally able to defeat the Huns around 530. But by that time the Gupta Empire was a mere shell of its former self. In the decades that followed it ceased to exist and history repeated itself, as once more India fragmented into many small and largely ineffectual states. Whatever dreams and ambitions the leaders of these states may have had, they and their successors faced a harsh reality: The magnificent empires that had dominated India's ancient era were gone forever.

Chapter Seven

Ancient Indian Society and Institutions

Modern scholars have learned about various aspects of ancient Indian life from a variety of sources. First, there is a fair amount of archaeological evidence, consisting of excavated streets, houses, hearths, furniture, tools, jewelry, coins, and numerous other artifacts. Archaeologists and other experts have also studied surviving ancient sculptures, which often show clothing and jewelry styles; religious beliefs and customs; social, political, and military practices; and much more. There are also some detailed descriptions of ancient Indian customs and institutions in surviving written documents, especially the *Arthashastra* and other documents from the Mauryan era.

These diverse sources reveal that ancient Indian society was not static and unchanging over the course of its dozens of centuries of existence. Houses and their contents, family life, clothing styles, craft and artistic styles, social customs, and the institutions, rules, and laws imposed by governments did change from age to age. Also affecting these aspects of daily life were the personal—particularly financial—circumstances of individuals and families. As in all times and places, nobles and other wealthy people had bigger, better-built homes, more belongings, finer clothes, and usually more social privileges and opportunities than those in the lower classes.

Yet overall life did not change dramatically over the course of India's ancient period. True, differences in lifestyle and social privilege always existed between rich and poor people, and laws and religious customs evolved somewhat from age to age. But overall there was a strong sense of tradition and continuity. And if a person could have magically transported from a city in one of the Mahajanapadas in 500 B.C. to the Gupta capital of Pataliputra a thousand years later, he or she could quickly and easily have learned to fit in. A visit to the central outdoor marketplace, for instance, would have been an almost identical experience in both times and places. French scholar Jeannine Auboyer describes the scene:

> Crowds of shoppers strolled along in front of the shelves piled high with green vegetables, fruits of all kinds [and] cooked rice and prepared foods ready for eating, whose pungent odors contrasted with the more delicate scents given off by the pyramids of incense sticks and sandalwood arranged on the perfumers' counters. Elsewhere, jewelers and goldsmiths cut and arranged precious stones and polished different metals, while . . . tailors cut and stitched garments, smiths hammered out copper vessels, [and] weavers worked their looms and sold materials. [Meanwhile] rich and poor, delivery men and shoppers, hirelings and porters, elbowed each other.[50]

Houses Big and Small

The kinds of houses these shoppers and merchants dwelled in varied somewhat according to when they were built, whether they were rural or urban, and the financial circumstances of the owners. Throughout India's ancient centuries, poor country folk, mostly subsistence farmers and laborers, typically lived in modest, one-story huts. These were made from dried mud and/or thatch (tightly bundled tree branches). Such a house usually had one or two small rooms, no

Artifacts, such as these Gupta coins, have helped scholars learn about various aspects of ancient Indian life.

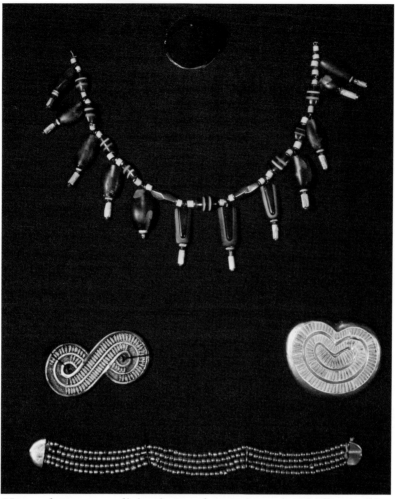

Upper-class women, living in townhouses in ancient India, would probably have worn jewelry like the pieces pictured here.

more than one window, and a dirt floor, sometimes overlaid by mats made of interwoven river reeds. There was little furniture. People sat on the floor, so chairs were not necessary. But there was often a bed, constructed of a bamboo framework with reed mats or other softer materials piled on top. The residents cooked their food in a crude fireplace fueled by wood and dried plants.

Such dwellings probably existed in large towns and cities, too. But their numbers, size, and features are unknown because they were made of very perishable materials and have left little or no trace in the archaeological record. What *has* survived from these ancient cities shows that many townhouses were larger and more comfortable. This is because their owners were middle-class workers,

The Family Gardens

Well-to-do townhouses in India's Gupta period almost always featured private gardens, described here by scholar Jeannine Auboyer.

The garden was looked after with great care. It contained a vegetable garden which the mistress of the house supervised personally and in which she grew the medicinal plants needed for treating the family's ailments. The rest of the garden was decorated with spreading trees, flowering shrubs, and banana-plants. The general effect was enhanced by a few ornamental pools whose sparkling surfaces were half-hidden by pink lotus-blossoms. . . . A swing was fixed up in some shady spot, from a tree branch or on a wooden platform, and adults as well as children used it from springtime onwards.

Jeannine Auboyer, *Daily Life in Ancient India*. London: Phoenix, 2002, p. 135.

such as craftsmen, artisans, or merchants; or upper-class nobles, courtiers, and rich traders. Members of these classes could afford houses made of wood or brick. Brick was used for residential structures mainly in the Harappan towns of the third and second millennia B.C. In contrast, wood and bamboo were the principal structural materials for townhouses in the Mauryan and Gupta periods.

A typical well-to-do townhouse in the fourth or fifth century A.D., for example, had two or three stories supported by a sturdy wooden framework. It had two entrances, one facing the street, the other opening into a private backyard containing gardens. The rooms were divided from one another not by solid walls, but by woven mats hung vertically from bam-boo poles set horizontally in the ceilings. Thus the layout of each story could be changed relatively easily by rearranging the poles and mats. Auboyer describes other aspects of construction and layout:

A veranda [terrace] with [wooden] columns shaded the ground floor and the other floors had balconies. The top story, under the eaves, used for storing the family's valuables and reserve provisions, was lighted by gable-windows whose brightly painted wooden frames could be seen and admired from the street. . . . The roofs themselves might be thatched, tiled, or shingled. Sometimes they were terraced instead and the family could then come up to enjoy the coolness of the night air and watch the stars. The windows were masked by lattice-work screens, by mats, or by curtains decorated with geometrical patterns. . . . [Also, ancient] texts allude to the existence of a secret chamber [or] compartment [where] the family treasure was hidden.[51]

Such comfortable homes featured plenty of furniture, including comfortable beds with pillows and sometimes canopies above. There were benches and small sofas for sitting and wooden tables on which women placed their makeup and toiletries or men played chess (which was invented in ancient India). The kitch-

This cave wall painting depicts family life during the Gupta dynasty from 320 to 600.

en was usually outside in the garden area. It consisted of a brick hearth for cooking and tables for preparing food, all sheltered from the sun and rain by a canopy held up by bamboo poles.

Family Roles and Marriage

The average house in ancient India was home to a large family (*kula*). Not much is known about family structure and customs in the Harappan and Vedic ages. But from the Mauryan era on, extended families were common. These included not only a father, mother, and their children, but also grandparents, aunts, uncles, and servants. Furthermore, an unknown proportion of families, particularly among the upper-class Kshatriyas, practiced polygamy. So the husband/father (*grhastha*), who was the head of the household, might have two or more wives, each of whom bore him children.

By custom, the *grhastha* had many crucial duties and roles. He made all the major decisions for the family, often after consulting with various relatives, perhaps including his wife. He also worked to earn the money needed to support the family, arranged marriages for his children, and oversaw religious worship in the home. For example, twice a day the father led the family in the performance of rituals at an in-house altar.

The wife/mother of a family had a lower social status and more limited freedom of movement than her husband. On the other hand she had almost complete authority over domestic affairs, including child-rearing, meal preparation, and the growing of herbs the family used for medicines. She was rarely allowed to leave the family compound, however; and when she did, to attend religious festivals or go on family outings, she was chaperoned by a male adult and had to wear a shawl over her body and a veil across her face.

Ancient Indian women were also subject to various punishments for a wide variety of infractions, some of them quite minor by modern standards. Some of these punishments took the form of beatings administered by their husbands or fathers. But there were also monetary fines for bad behavior that were levied by a council of community elders. According to the *Arthashastra*:

> If a woman engages herself in amorous sports [flirting?], or drinking in the face of an order to the contrary, she shall be fined 3 *panas*. She shall pay a fine of 6 *panas* for going out at day time [unchaperoned] to see a woman [friend]. . . . She shall pay a fine of 12 *panas* if she goes out to see another man [and] for the same offences committed at night, the fines shall be doubled. . . . If a man and a woman make signs to each other with a view to sensual enjoyment, or carry on secret conversation (for the same purpose), the woman shall pay a fine of 24 *panas,* and the man, double the amount.[52]

In contrast, for a woman in Mauryan or Gupta society her marriage day was a major high point of her life. She wore a beautiful dress and took part in a splendid

A Gupta-style wall painting of a princess and her servant. From Mauryan times on, a majority of middle- and upper-class families owned slaves.

wedding ceremony and feast attended by hundreds of people. Before the marriage (*vivaha*), her father had paid her future husband a dowry (*sulka*), money or valuables to help support her in the marriage. It was common for a father to promise his daughter to a suitor when she was only eight, nine, or ten, even if the wedding itself did not take place until later. Ten to fourteen was a common marriage age for girls; boys were usually a little older. Because marriage was viewed as a sacred institution, divorce was rare.

Slaves: Their Duties and Privileges

Another institution that affected the family was slavery, since from Mauryan times on, a majority of middle- and upper-class families owned slaves. People obtained slaves in several ways. Some were prisoners taken during wars fought among Indian states; others were foreigners bought by Indian merchants, who then sold them to Indian customers; and still others were children born to slaves who were already part of a family. In addition it was possible for a person to sell him- or herself into slavery on a temporary basis as a way of settling a debt. Kautilya's *Arthashastra* mentions punishments meted out to debt-slaves who committed crimes:

> Any person who has once voluntarily enslaved himself shall, if guilty of an offence, be a slave for life. Similarly, any person whose life has been twice mortgaged by others shall, if guilty of an offence, be a slave for life.[53]

Evidence suggests that life for most ancient Indian slaves was hard but not unbearable or hopeless. They did have to do difficult menial labor, such as carrying the family water from a stream, fountain, or other water source to the house. But many of their duties were lighter—for example helping the lady of the household clean, prepare meals, and garden. Also, though slaves could be beaten for breaking rules or laziness, the severity of punishments was often limited by law. Moreover, Mauryan law actually imposed

Religious Architecture

Because religion was among the most important social institutions in ancient India, governments and communities put a great deal of time and money into erecting temples that both glorified the gods and inspired awe and devotion in worshipers. The most basic form of these temples, which began to appear in the first millennium B.C., was the stupa. It began as a circular earthen burial mound. But over time people transformed stupas into dome-shaped temples constructed of fired bricks or stone blocks that were often plastered and painted. They also added circular walls, fences, or other enclosures around stupas, some of which became very large and elaborate. Among the more outstanding examples is the Great Stupa at Sanchi, a Buddhist temple in north-central India. Still in good condition, it is 120 feet (37m) across and 54 feet (15.5m) high. Hindu temples also utilized the stupa form, though often in more developed adaptations. These included the shikhara, a pagoda-like tower that was essentially a stupa extended upward for several stories. Hindu temples, especially from the Gupta period onward, were typically adorned, both inside and out, with elaborate, sometimes crowded displays of statues and other sculptures depicting the gods and their legendary deeds.

fines, some of them heavy, on owners who mistreated their slaves. According to Kautilya:

> Employing a slave [only] to carry the dead or to sweep manure [or] urine; [or] keeping a slave naked; or hurting or abusing him . . . shall cause the forfeiture of the value paid for him or her. . . . When a man commits or helps another to commit rape with a . . . female slave pledged to him, he shall not only forfeit the purchase value, but also pay a certain amount of money to her and a fine of twice that amount to the government.[54]

Another benefit that Indian slaves had was the right to earn money. With his or her master's permission, a slave could do work outside the home and be paid for it. Moreover the slave could save up this money and, if the master was willing, buy his or her freedom. Some masters also allowed their female slaves to marry free men and live in these men's homes; the condition was that such a women had to return to the master's house each day and perform certain chores.

Taxation and Other Government Institutions

Everyday life in the Mauryan and Gupta eras was shaped by more than traditional social institutions such as religion, family, marriage, and slavery. There were also governmental institutions, rules, and practices that affected people of all social classes and castes. For instance, just as people in nearly every modern nation

must pay taxes on a routine basis, the ancient Indians had a similar obligation. In fact the Mauryans' and Guptas' huge administrative bureaucracies and armies could not have been maintained without large-scale tax collection, and the office of revenue and taxation was one of the biggest departments of the Mauryan government. It was highly organized, with thousands of officials, tax collectors, and clerks working in every corner of the empire and all reporting back to a central authority.

Among the most lucrative taxes were tolls levied on all manner of trade goods, from food and drink to clothing, craftwares, building materials, and more. The toll collectors set up booths at all town and city gates and inspected every person and pack animal seeking entry. "When merchants with their merchandise arrive at the toll-gate," Kautilya wrote,

> four or five collectors shall take down who the merchants are, whence they come, what amount of merchandise they have brought and where for the first time the [official government] sealmark has been made on the merchandise. Those whose merchandise has not been stamped with sealmark shall pay twice the amount of toll. . . . Imported commodities shall pay

An elephant statue stands outside a Jain shrine. Mauryan kings were deeply concerned about certain kinds of wildlife preservation, especially elephants, and stated that anyone who killed an elephant would be put to death.

1/5th of their value as toll. Of flower, fruit, vegetables, roots, seeds, dried fish, and dried meat, the superintendent shall receive 1/6th as toll. . . . Of cloths, four-footed beasts, two-legged beasts, threads, cotton, scents, medicines, wood, bamboo . . . clay-pots, grains, oils, sugar, salt, liquor, cooked rice, and the like, he shall receive 1/20th or 1/25th as toll.[55]

Another way the government exercised control over people's lives was by closely and secretly watching them. Despite their largely humane approach to rule, the Mauryan kings, including A oka, maintained a large network of spies (cara). According to the Arthashatra:

Spies under the disguise of house-holders [verify claims made about such things as] the area and output of [farmers'] fields, right of ownership and remission of taxes with regard to houses, and the caste and profession regarding families. They shall also . . . find out the causes of emigration and immigration of [all native Indians], as well as the movements of foreign spies.[56]

The government also maintained numerous constructive institutions that promoted the welfare of the citizenry and even local wildlife. There were plans in place for avoiding large death tolls and alleviating suffering during national

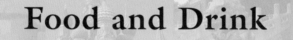

Food and Drink

The ancient Indians consumed a wide range of nutritious foods. Not much is known about the eating habits of the Harappans and early Vedic people. But some evidence shows that they grew barley, wheat, rice, peas, melons, and dates; fished; and raised sheep, pigs, and cattle. After the spread of Buddhism and Jainism, both of which discourage the killing of animals, meat-eating became much less common. Some people, particularly among the Kshatriya caste, still ate meat, but never from animals that give milk; so foul and fish were acceptable. By the Gupta era most Indians were vegetarians. Rice was a mainstay of the diet, including thick soups made of rice and vegetables, and rice flour, which people used to make bread-pancakes (capati) that are still widely popular in India today. Other important food staples included barley, wheat, beans (which were both boiled and fried), many varieties of vegetables and fruits, and honey and sugar cane for sweeteners. The most common drinks were water and milk. But many adults also drank alcoholic beverages made by fermenting coconuts, rice, or barley.

disasters, for example. Edicts with the force of law instructed people on what to do in case of floods, fires, disease epidemics, famine, rat infestations, and so forth. And the king pledged to feed the populace during famines and other catastrophes.

In addition the same rulers maintained public lands that combined the modern concepts of game preserve and national forest. The Mauryan kings, for instance, were deeply concerned about certain kinds of wildlife preservation, especially the nurture of elephants. "Wild tracts shall be separated from timber-forests," Kautilya wrote.

In the extreme limit of the country, elephant forests, separated from wild tracts, shall be formed. The superintendent of forests with his retinue of forest guards shall . . . maintain the up-keep of the forests [and] whoever kills an elephant shall be put to death.[57]

These and other well-meaning, beneficial government institutions were among the factors that ranked India's Mauryan and Gupta societies among the most advanced and enlightened in the ancient world.

Ancient India's Legacy

Ancient India's principal legacy was a large and rich collection of cultural and religious ideas and customs that affected the development of all later dynasties, states, and ethnic and political groups in the subcontinent. The Hindu faith is a clear example. Born long ago in the Vedic Age, it survived the fall of the Mauryans, Kushans, Guptas, and other ancient dynasties. Hinduism also remained intact in India during and after a series of later invasions by peoples who practiced Islam. Today the Hindu faith, with nearly all of its ancient beliefs and customs intact, ranks among the world's leading religions.

The Muslim Incursions

In a like manner, in all the centuries following the demise of the Gupta Empire, India never ceased to be a huge, diverse region with expansive human and material resources. And as in the past, this continued to make it enormously attractive to outsiders hoping to exploit it. The first major post-Gupta foreign incursions were those of various Muslim groups. These were successful mainly because most of the Indian kingdoms that had replaced the Gupta Empire were relatively weak and disunited.

The initial Muslim intrusion in the 600s was little more than a large-scale raid and had no lasting effect on Indian culture. But a larger incursion in the period of 980 to 1030 created a Muslim base in the Punjab. Furthermore a still larger thrust that began in the late 1100s succeeded in setting up a large Muslim state in northern India. Called the Delhi Sultanate, it lasted from 1206 to 1526 and featured several dynamic dynasties of rulers. Meanwhile soon after 1400 a number of other Islamic rulers established kingdoms in northern India.

All of these early Muslim-ruled Indian states eventually fell to a new wave of invaders—the Timurids (Sunni Muslims of Asian-Mongol descent). In 1526 the leader of the Timurids, Zahir-ud-Din Muhammad (known as Babur, or "tiger, lion, or panther"), established the Mughal dynasty and empire. The Mughals managed to gain control of most of northern India by about 1600, during the reign of Babur's grandson, Jalal ud-Din Muhammad Akbar.

With a few exceptions the Mughals, especially Akbar, were tolerant of Hinduism, which continued to be practiced by a majority of Indians. Neither did these rulers impose strictly Muslim artistic styles on the country; rather, they respected and promoted a wide range of styles. The famous Taj Mahal, in Agra (in northern India), is a prominent example. Completed in 1648 it was built by the Mughal emperor Shah Jahan as a mausoleum for his beloved wife. This splendid structure is illustrative of the cultural fusion that occurred in the Mughal Age because it combines elements of Persian, Indian, Islamic, and other architectural styles.

The Coming of the British

In the early 1700s the Mughal Empire began to decline, in part because a number of smaller states arose in various parts of the subcontinent and challenged Mughal power. Chief among these rivals was the Maratha Confederacy, centered in its capital of Pune, in southwestern

Mughal ruins in Delhi, India. The Mughal empire managed to gain control of most of northern India by about 1600, but began to decline by the early 1700s.

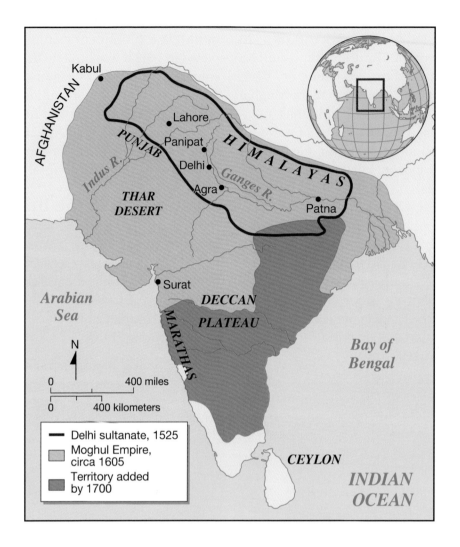

Kabul

AFGHANISTAN

Lahore

PUNJAB

Panipat

Indus R.

Delhi

HIMALAYAS

THAR
DESERT

Agra

Ganges R.

Patna

Surat

*Arabian
Sea*

DECCAN

PLATEAU

MARATHAS

N

Bay of
Bengal

0   400 miles

0   400 kilometers

CEYLON

INDIAN
OCEAN

Delhi sultanate, 1525
Moghul Empire,
circa 1605
Territory added
by 1700

India. During this period of infighting among Indian states, another foreign power—Britain—was making inroads into the subcontinent, at first strictly through trade. With the permission of the Mughal rulers, the British East India Company set up trading posts in India in the 1600s.

But as the company's economic base steadily expanded, it began using hired soldiers—a mix of Europeans and native Indians (called sepoys)—to enforce its will. The company took over the Bengal region in the 1750s and 1760s and thereafter continued to expand its influence, largely at the expense of the Mughals, Marathas, and other native Indians. Rising discontent among Indians over the company's expanding power, coupled with the continued decline of Mughal power, led to the Indian Rebellion (or Sepoy Mutiny) of 1857. Although the native rebels fought courageously, the company's forces, reinforced by thousands of regular British troops, crushed them.

The British government in London now saw that the East India Company had accumulated far too much power. So it promptly abolished the company and instituted direct British control over most of the subcontinent; British rule in India subsequently became known as the British Raj. Among Britain's many colonies around the world at the time, India was by far its most productive and financially lucrative. So the British were very reluctant to part with the region, which they came to call "the jewel in the crown" (meaning the British monarch's crown).

India Gains Its Independence

But no matter how valuable India was to Britain, the right of self-rule was even more important to the Indians. In 1885, not long after the establishment of the Raj, several prominent Indians formed the Indian National Congress. Its goal was to work toward establishing independence from the British. At first what became known as the Indian Independence Movement made little progress. But this began to change shortly before 1920 with the emergence of a brilliant and courageous Indian political activist named Mohandas Gandhi. He advocated a strategy of relentless nonviolent protests, many of which he personally led, along with the boycotting of British goods.

Although it took many years, this approach worked. In 1946 the British agreed to grant India its independence the following year. However, by this time members of the large Muslim minority worried that their rights in the new country would be suppressed by the Hindu majority. So Muslim leaders called for the partition, or division, of India into two new countries, one ruled by Muslims, the other by Hindus. Thus in August 1947 the two nations—Pakistan and the Republic of India—were established. (At first Muslim Pakistan was divided into two sections—West Pakistan, centered in the Indus Valley, and East Pakistan, situated north of the Bay of Bengal. But in 1971 East Pakistan forcibly broke away and became the independent nation of Bangladesh.)

Since gaining its independence and establishing a democracy, India has made enormous strides in an effort to modernize and financially compete with other large, populous nations, including China, Russia, and the United States. In the 1950s and 1960s, for instance, the Indians expanded women's civil rights, built thousands of new schools, and passed laws banning discrimination against members of the lower castes. They also built many new roads, dams, canals, and electric power plants. What is more in 1974 India acquired nuclear weapons, making it one of only six nations that had such weapons at the time. The 1990s witnessed the emergence of telecommunications and information technology industries in India that have become extremely successful in global markets.

In spite of these modern advances, however, India has not lost its ties with its long and eventful past. It still retains

Mohandas Gandhi was an Indian political activist who advocated nonviolent protests as a means of gaining India's independence from Britain.

many of the cultural, artistic, linguistic, literary, and religious ideas that originated in the subcontinent in ancient times. These surviving aspects of ancient India's legacy are the ultimate proof that conti-nuity and reverence for tradition have been the main forces that have guided the Indian people through the long and twisting corridors of their history.

Notes

Introduction: A Nation in Touch with Its Past

1. Sinharaja Tammita-Delgoda, *A Traveller's History of India*. New York: Interlink, 2003, p. 1.
2. Alain Danielou, *A Brief History of India*. Rochester, VT: Inner Traditions, 2003, p. v.
3. Tammita-Delgoda, *A Traveller's History of India*, p. 1.

Chapter 1: India's Earliest Inhabitants

4. Tammita-Delgoda, *A Traveller's History of India*, p. 14.
5. Bridget and Raymond Allchin, *The Birth of Indian Civilization. Harmondsworth, UK: Penguin*, 1968, p. 131.
6. Gordon Johnson, *Cultural Atlas of India*. New York: Facts on File, 1996, p. 62.
7. Tammita-Delgoda, *A Traveller's History of India*, p. 21.
8. John Keay, *India: A History*. New York: Grove, 2000, pp. 8–9.
9. Tammita-Delgoda, *A Traveller's History of India*, p. 24.
10. Tammita-Delgoda, *A Traveller's History of India*, pp. 31–32.

Chapter 2: The Aryans and the Vedic Age

11. B.B. Lal, "Why Perpetuate Myths? A Fresh Look at Indian History." http://www.geocities.com/ifihhome/articles/bbl002.html
12. Keay, *India*, p. 22.
13. Quoted in Lal, "Why Perpetuate Myths?"
14. Also translated as "fortress-destroyer." See Rig-Veda, Book 8, Hymn 1, line 7, trans. Ralph T.H. Griffith. http://www.sacred-texts.com/hin/rigveda/rv08001.htm.
15. Keay, *India*, pp. 21–22.
16. G.F. Dales, "The Mythical Massacre at Mohenjo-Daro," in Gregory L. Possehl, ed., *Ancient Cities of the Indus*. New Delhi: Vikas, 1979, p. 293.
17. Lal, "Why Perpetuate Myths?"
18. David Frawley, "The Myth of the Aryan Invasion of India." http://www.hindunet.org/hindu_history/ancient/aryan/aryan_frawley.html.
19. Keay, *India*, pp. 28–29.

Chapter 3: Invasions from the West

20. Herodotus, *The Histories*, trans. Aubrey de Sélincourt. New York: Penguin, 1972, p. 284.
21. Herodotus, *The Histories*, p. 285.
22. Herodotus, *The Histories*, pp. 467, 471.
23. Keay, *India*, pp. 71–72.
24. Arrian, *Anabasis Alexandri*, published as *The Campaigns of Alexander*, trans.

Aubrey de Sélincourt. New York: Penguin, 1971, pp. 267, 269.

25. Arrian, *The Campaigns of Alexander*, pp. 277–278.

26. Arrian, *The Campaigns of Alexander*, pp. 279–280.

27. Quoted in Arrian, *The Campaigns of Alexander*, p. 281.

Chapter 4: The Mauryan Empire

28. Tammita-Delgoda, *A Traveller's History of India*, p. 55.

29. Quintus Curtius Rufus, *History of Alexander*, trans. John Yardley. New York: Penguin, 1984, p. 215.

30. Quoted in Danielou, *A Brief History of India*, p. 70.

31. Plutarch, *Life of Alexander*, in *The Age of Alexander: Nine Greek Lives by Plutarch*, trans. Ian Scott-Kilvert. New York: Penguin, 1973, p. 319.

32. Keay, *India*, p. 83.

33. Kautilya, *Arthashastra*, Book 1, trans. R. Shamasastry. http://www.mssu.edu/projectsouthasia/history/primarydocs/Arthashastra/BookI.htm.

34. Megasthenes, *Indika*, surviving fragments collected in J.W. McCrindle, ed. and trans., *Ancient India Described by Megasthenes and Arrian*. Calcutta: Tracker, Spink, 1877, excerpted at: htttp://www.mssu.edu/projectsouthasia/history/primarydocs/Foreign_Views/GreekRoman/Megasthenes-Indika.htm.

35. Aśoka's 13th Rock Inscription, in "The Edicts of King Ashoka," trans. Ven S. Dhammika.

http://www.cs.colostate.edu/~malaiya/ashoka.html.

36. Aśoka's 2nd and 3rd Pillar Edicts, in "The Edicts of King Ashoka."

37. Aśoka's 12th Rock Inscription, in "The Edicts King of Ashoka."

38. Keay, *India*, p. 100.

Chapter 5: India's Three Great Religions

39. Rig-Veda, Book 1, Hymn 25, trans. Ralph T.H. Griffith. http://www.sacred-texts.com/hin/rigveda/rv01025.htm.

40. Tammita-Delgoda, *A Traveller's History of India*, p. 48.

41. Quoted in Lin Yutang, ed., *The Wisdom of China and India*. New York: Random House, 1955, p. 360.

42. John Bowker, *World Religions*. London: Dorling Kindersley, 1997, p. 42.

Chapter 6: The Guptas and the Golden Age

43. Keay, *India*, p. 111.

44. Keay, *India*, p. 117.

45. Quoted in Tammita-Delgoda, *A Traveller's History of India*, p. 76.

46. Tammita-Delgoda, *A Traveller's History of India*, p. 78.

47. Fa-hsien, *Record of the Buddhist Kingdoms*, chap. 27, trans. James Legge. http://www.gutenberg.org/dirs/2/1/2/2124/2124.txt

48. Fa-hsien, *Record of the Buddhist Kingdoms*, chap. 27.

49. *Kalidasa, The Birth of the War God*, trans. Arthur W. Ryder. http://www.sacred-texts.com/hin/sha/sha16.htm.

Chapter 7: Ancient Indian Society and Institutions

50. Jeannine Auboyer, *Daily Life in Ancient India*. London: Phoenix, 2002, pp. 121–122.
51. Auboyer, *Daily Life in Ancient India*, p. 133.
52. Kautilya, *Arthashastra*, Book 3, trans. R. Shamasastry. http://www.mssu.edu/projectsouthasia/history/primarydocs/Arthashastra/BookIII.htm.
53. Kautilya, *Arthashastra*, Book 3.
54. Kautilya, *Arthashastra*, Book 3.
55. Kautilya, *Arthashastra*, Book 2, trans. R. Shamasastry. http://www.mssu.edu/projectsouthasia/history/primarydocs/Arthashastra/BookII.htm.
56. Kautilya, *Arthashastra*, Book 2.
57. Kautilya, *Arthashastra*, Book 2.

For More Information

Books

Jeannine Auboyer, *Daily Life in Ancient India*. London: Phoenix, 2002. An informative look at ancient Indian society, religion, family life, crafts, and more, from about 200 B.C. to A.D. 700.

A.L. Basham, *The Wonder That Was India*. New Delhi: Rupa, 1981. One of the best modern studies of India and its history.

James Heitzman and Robert L. Worden, *India: A Country Study*. Washington, DC: U.S. Government Printing Office, 1996. A complete collection of facts about all aspects of India, including its history from ancient to modern times.

John Keay, *India: A History*. New York: Grove, 2000. Widely viewed as one of the most important historical studies of India in English; highlighted by numerous color photos.

Gregory L. Possehl, *Harappan Civilization*. Oxford: IBH, 1993. This excellent overview of India's first civilization is only slightly dated and remains useful and authoritative.

Steven J. Rosen, *Essential Hinduism*. New York: Praeger, 2006. A very informative synopsis of one of the three great religions that began in ancient India.

Benjamin Rowland, *The Art and Architecture of India*. New York: Penguin, 1981.

Part of the respected Pelican History of Art series, this is a well-informed, well-illustrated introduction to the subject.

Virginia Schomp, *Ancient India*. New York: Franklin Watts, 2005. A well-written general introduction to ancient Indian history and culture for younger readers.

Vincent A. Smith, *The Oxford History of India*. New York: Oxford University Press, 1981. A sturdy overview of the subject.

Burton Stein, *A History of India*. Oxford: Blackwell, 1998. A detailed, well-researched study of India's march of civilizations, this one has a particularly strong section on the Harappans.

Sinharaja Tammita-Delgoda, *A Traveller's History of India*. New York: Interlink, 2003. A very useful brief overview of Indian history and culture.

Internet

Battle of Hydaspes http://joseph_berrigan.tripod.com/ancientbabylon/id36.html. An excellent, easy-to-read overview of the battle in which Alexander the Great defeated the Indian king Porus, this site has numerous color pictures.

Buddhism http://www.bbc.co.uk/religion/religions/buddhism/. Provided by the BBC, this useful site provides links to dozens of sites explaining all aspects of the faith.

Daily Life in Ancient India http://members.aol.com/Donnclass/Indialife.html. A kid-friendly site that examines the basics of ancient Indian life. Also includes links to other aspects of Indian culture.

Indian Language and Literature http://www.historyforkids.org/learn/india/literature/index.htm. A short overview with several links to sites about important Indian religious writings, including the Rig Veda and Ramayana.

Jainism http://www.bbc.co.uk/religion/religions/jainism/. Excellent BBC-sponsored site with loads of links to useful blurbs about this important ancient Indian religion.

The Mauryans http://www.wsu.edu/~dee/ANCINDIA/ANCINDIA.HTM. A good brief overview of the dynasty that created the largest empire in Indian history.

Myth of the Aryan Invasion http://www.gosai.com/chaitanya/ashrama/links/aryan-invasion-fs.html. A well-written general look at the traditional theory about the Aryan invasion of India, with recent arguments and evidence that call that theory into question.

Index

Picture Credits

About the Author

Historian Don Nardo has written extensively about the ancient world. His many studies of ancient Greece and Rome include *Life in Ancient Athens, The Age of Augustus, Greek and Roman Sport, Life of a Roman Gladiator;* and Greenhaven Press's encyclopedias of ancient Greece, ancient Rome, and Greek and Roman mythology. Mr. Nardo has also produced volumes about ancient Egypt, ancient Mesopotamia, and ancient Japan. He lives with wife Christine in Massachusetts.